T0340487

Happy
Skin
Kitchen

Happy Skin Kitchen

Over 100 recipes to
nourish your skin
from the inside out

Elisa Rossi

HarperCollins*Publishers*

HarperCollins*Publishers*
1 London Bridge Street
London SE1 9GF

www.harpercollins.co.uk

HarperCollins*Publishers*
Macken House,
39/40 Mayor Street Upper,
Dublin 1, D01 C9W8
Ireland

First published by HarperCollins*Publishers* 2023

1 3 5 7 9 10 8 6 4 2

Text © Elisa Rossi 2023
Recipe photography © Elisa Rossi 2023, except for the
following pages, © Rebecca Hincke; pp. 138, 141, 172, 201,
203, 213
All other photographs © Dan Jones 2023
Design and layout by Nikki Ellis Design

Elisa Rossi asserts the moral right to be identified
as the author of this work

A catalogue record of this book is available from
the British Library

ISBN 978-0-00-853091-4

Printed and bound by GPS Group, Slovenia

All rights reserved. No part of this publication may be
reproduced, stored in a retrieval system, or transmitted,
in any form or by any means, electronic, mechanical,
photocopying, recording or otherwise, without the prior
written permission of the publishers.

The author of this work has made every effort to ensure that the information contained in this
book is as accurate and up-to-date as possible at the time of publication. It is recommended that
readers always consult a qualified medical specialist for individual advice, this book should not
be used as an alternative to seeking specialist medical advice which should be sought before any
action is taken. The author and publishers cannot be held responsible for any errors and omissions
that may be found in the text, or any actions that may be taken by a reader as a result of any
reliance on the information contained in the text which is taken entirely at the reader's own risk.

This book is produced from independently certified FSC™
paper to ensure responsible forest management.

For more information visit: www.harpercollins.co.uk/green

WHEN USING KITCHEN APPLIANCES PLEASE ALWAYS FOLLOW
THE MANUFACTURER'S INSTRUCTIONS

Foreword

I'm a registered Nutritional Therapist and I help busy people look and feel good. I started my career working in the sales department of technology companies and although I enjoyed the work, I definitely empathize with Elisa's experience of burning the candle at both ends and eventually not feeling like myself. One year into that career I decided to pursue my passion of nutrition and I studied for four years at the prestigious Institute for Optimum Nutrition in London, alongside my job.

Since qualifying, I see 1:1 clients in my virtual private practice, run workshops for companies and write on various nutrition topics. I absolutely love what I do, so when Elisa reached out to me I immediately recognized her passion for healthy living. We spoke for hours about our ethos when it comes to nutrition and lifestyle and within five minutes I had a gut feeling that I wanted to be involved with this project.

Before I studied nutrition I thought that healthy eating meant consuming low calorie foods. I didn't have an awareness around the importance of nutrients, fibre and variety. Unfortunately, this belief is something I see all the time in clinical practice. On the whole, there is a real lack of nutrition knowledge. This is totally understandable as for the most part we are not taught about nutrition at school, doctors receive on average about eight hours of nutrition training and the government does not seem to offer much in the way of education in schools. Nowadays, people learn about nutrition through social media and news articles which can be confusing, sensationalist and dangerous.

This is one reason why reading through Elisa's book has been extremely enjoyable. Elisa advocates for whole foods to nourish the skin and body from the inside out and explains their benefits related to skin health. This is a book bursting with healthy recipes, but the focus is on enjoyment and abundance rather than deprivation. This is a real step in the right direction as clearly the latter option does not suffice.

There is no doubt that skincare is having a real moment. A new skincare brand seems to pop up every other day. While the skincare industry is fascinating, we cannot ignore the fact that the most effective way we can care for our skin is from the inside out. You can spend hundreds of pounds on skincare each month, but if you're consuming an ultra-processed diet lacking in nutrients and plant diversity, there is only so much you can do.

Every day we are presented with a choice: do we consume food and drink that nourishes our body, or do we consume that which does the opposite? Of course, as Elisa so eloquently discusses in the book, there is room in a healthy diet for occasional sweet treats, takeaways and the like. However, in order to feel and look our best, the bulk of our diet should be full of nutrient-dense whole foods.

I love how Elisa constantly weaves in the benefit of cooking more than you need, so you can have leftovers in the coming days. Not only will this save you time, it will also save you money. Try to set some time aside each week to make a few recipes from this book, and your future self will thank you. Not only are they delicious, they are also packed full of nutrient-dense ingredients and are quick to prepare. The Creamy Cannellini, Mushroom & Cavolo Nero Stew and the Almond Butter & Miso Shiitake Mushroom Bowl are favourites of mine. If you're looking to nourish your skin from the inside out, you are in for a treat with these recipes.

Sophie Trotman
DipION mBANT CNHC

Contents

About Me

This is my story: my struggle with hormonal acne and how adopting a plant-based diet finally cleared my skin. You might not realize it, but your skin is actually your biggest organ. The importance of keeping your skin healthy can't be emphasized enough. Its main function is to act as a barrier to prevent pathogens, nasties and other harmful agents penetrating your body, but it also regulates body temperature, maintains fluid balance and controls moisture loss.

Your skin also provides a good indication of what's going on with your overall health. I look at my skin as a mirror to what's happening inside my body. When our digestion, hormones, immune system or blood sugar levels are out of balance, this will often show up on our skin in the form of acne, rosacea, eczema and more. I am a firm believer that maintaining healthy skin is an inside-out process and what we feed ourselves has a deep impact on how we look.

I grew up in a small village in the countryside near Bologna, in the north of Italy. I had a pretty idyllic childhood, with green fields, woodland and rivers as my playground. My dad has always been passionate about sustainability and organic farming and 90 per cent of the fresh produce we ate came from my dad's abundant vegetable garden and fruit orchards. Growing up in rural Italy in the 90s also meant that fast food, convenience and ultra-processed foods weren't really part of my life. Don't get me wrong, I had cakes, pastries and crisps at birthday parties but they were always once-in-a-while events, never a daily or weekly occurrence. My mum was the cook of the house. On Sundays she would always batch-cook a big jar of tomato sauce or trays of lasagne or meatballs with peas, which we would live off throughout the week.

Even though eating your 5-a-day wasn't a big thing back in those days, my parents always made us eat our vegetables and salad. It was non-negotiable. My brother and I had to scoff down bowls of vegetables before we could eat our pasta or whatever was on the menu that day. Like most children, I didn't particularly love vegetables, eating them was a chore more than anything else. However, I always loved food! I was never a picky eater and I always loved my mum and grandma's cooking. Looking back, I now realize how lucky I was to have freshly cooked meals, made with love, especially when they used my dad's home-grown organic produce.

I wholeheartedly loved my childhood in the countryside but when I hit the teenage years, living in such a rural environment started to feel almost suffocating. I worked in bars and restaurants to pay my way during my university years in the city of Bologna, but I was already dreaming about travelling and living in a big, exciting city, so after graduating university I took the leap and moved to London.

At 22 I was freshly arrived in London and busy living my 'best life'. I was doing my first internship at a PR agency. I was meeting new people, staying out late, drinking more than I probably should have been, and in general I was just having fun in this big, bright, new city, which I fell in love with immediately. And then my skin started to break out. I was 23 by then so it was unexpected as I thought the teenage acne years were firmly behind me. Like most people, I'd experienced a few spots as a teenager, however these new breakouts were something altogether different. They were red, angry cysts sitting right under my skin, mostly on my chin and jaw area. Painful and often arriving in gangs of two or three they would happily sit on my face for weeks on end, and if I tried to squeeze them I would scar, which would then take even longer to heal. I was honestly at a loss as to how to remedy the issue.

As a young girl with limited funds, away from my family, and not knowing where to turn, my immediate reaction was to run to the nearest pharmacy and buy every single anti-acne product I could get my hands on. I thought, surely that will work, right? Unfortunately, I was proved tremendously wrong as my acne, if anything, got worse. All these products just made my skin drier and more inflamed, and they definitely didn't prevent my spots reappearing.

Next, I went to a dermatologist, to see if a qualified medical professional would be able to help me. Before I moved to London, I had stopped taking the contraceptive pill which I had been using on and off for years. The dermatologist recommended that I went back on the contraceptive pill. He told me that my hormones were probably out of balance and that the pill was probably the quickest and most effective solution. At the time I didn't think twice. If the pill guaranteed that those horrible, angry spots would finally leave, sign me up! As the dermatologist advised, it worked brilliantly. After many months of constant breakouts, scarring and many tears, my skin was finally clear! I was elated, so I carried on taking the contraceptive pill for another year. However, at the back of my mind I kept thinking that I couldn't be on the pill for the rest of my life, it wasn't feasible.

Hoping that the breakouts might have just been a phase and were now a thing of the past, eventually I decided to come off the pill again. How wrong I was. As soon as I stopped my cystic acne came back with a vengeance. My spots this time were bigger, redder and even more painful. I remember feeling so disheartened. I knew I had to get to the root cause of my acne once and for all. I could see that the contraceptive pill was just masking the symptoms without providing a real cure, so I took the medical route once again and over the next two years visited two dermatologists who prescribed me two different antibiotics, promising that they would eventually clear

my skin. I took each course of antibiotics religiously, and although I saw some improvement in the first few months, eventually my skin started to break out again and at the end of those two years I was back to square one, if not in a much worse situation. My skin was angry and inflamed, my bank account had been drained by all the private appointments plus the cost of the medication and my gut microbiome was depleted after taking antibiotics for so long. I had never felt so hopeless.

I almost gave up on my skin, thinking that maybe my fate was to have acne for the rest of my life and there was nothing I could do about it. Luckily my stubborn Italian blood won over, and after wiping away many frustrated tears I turned to our good friend Gary Google. I spent hours and hours researching, reading, watching videos, devouring anything I could find on how to clear acne through a diet and lifestyle approach. It became clear to me that if I ever wanted to heal my acne, something greater had to change. It wasn't just about a quick fix. I realized that rather than relying on specialists, treatments, products, prescriptions, pills and creams, I could take responsibility and control of my own skin – through my diet.

I followed experts, doctors and nutritionists from across the health spectrum, not just mainstream channels. I read books about skin, gut, exercise, mental health, diet, plant-based versus meat, dairy versus non-dairy, and so much more. I didn't suddenly have the answers, but I could relate to a lot of what I was reading, and it seemed to be common sense. I was eager to put parts of it into practice to get my clear skin back. My mindset had changed. I didn't have to wait for other people to give me answers, I could make positive changes myself.

A whole new world suddenly opened up to me; I couldn't believe that I had completely overlooked my diet for so long. I had been so focused on finding the 'magic cure' that I hadn't thought twice about what I was feeding myself three times a day, every day. My body and my skin were screaming for help and I had the visible scars to prove it. The main problem was that I didn't actually know how to cook. Although I have always loved food, cooking for myself was never top of my priority list. I was pretty spoiled as my mum, aunties and grandmas constantly cooked an assortment of Italian classics for me to gorge on. A regular Sunday lunch would consist of at least three courses, two of which would be pasta! Both my grandmas were known as the lasagne queens – they each had their own unique recipes and I always had one of their dishes stashed in the freezer.

I also had my wonderful aunt Irene, who always brought us freshly baked tigelle. These local delicacies are thin round discs of bread, almost a cross between a flatbread and an English muffin. A very popular street food in Emilia-Romagna, they are usually stuffed with meats or veg. Irene would also bring jars of fragrant pesto when basil was in season, and her signature homemade pizza, which even when cold was a feast for my taste buds. Outside of Italian food, though, I had lived a pretty sheltered life, especially considering the myriad cuisines available on my doorstep in London.

In my busy 20-something London life, preparing a meal for one felt like too much effort, especially after a long day at work and with a tempting takeaway menu available at the click of a finger. A ready-made pasta sauce and a bag of spaghetti was about as adventurous as I got. Looking back, I can see that feeding myself properly wasn't a priority. I didn't value it as something I should invest time in. But I was ready to make some serious changes to my diet and lifestyle. And so, my culinary, health and skin journey began!

"I never set out to be fully plant-based. I am Italian, after all, so the idea of giving up Parma ham and Parmesan cheese filled me with absolute dread, but the more I researched, the more I was pointed towards the incredible health benefits of a whole food plant-based diet, especially when it came to healing and managing hormonal acne."

I never set out to be fully plant-based. I am Italian, after all, so the idea of giving up Parma ham and Parmesan cheese filled me with dread, but the more I researched the more the incredible health benefits of a whole food plant-based diet became clear, especially when it came to healing and managing hormonal acne. I was so desperate to see some improvement in my skin that I was ready to give anything a go. However, I wanted this to be a sustainable lifestyle change, not just a fad diet. I wouldn't last a day if I went cold turkey and started eating kale and brown rice at every meal. So I started with small steps, focusing on increasing the amount of whole food plant-based foods I was consuming. That way, it felt more sustainable and less daunting.

I started by changing my breakfast, which in those days consisted of a full-fat cappuccino and croissant from Starbucks, eaten on the Tube on my way to work, or a bowl of cereal at home if I had some extra time. I made overnight oats for breakfast so I had something nourishing and delicious ready to go in the morning. I ate my oats while I was sitting on the Tube, and I remember thinking: 'This is actually pretty delicious and it took me 5 minutes to make – I can do this!' That jar of overnight oats was just the beginning of a whole diet and lifestyle overhaul. It snowballed into a newfound passion for cooking and nourishing myself and I began to spend my Sunday evenings meal-prepping recipes for the week ahead. I went to markets to find the freshest produce. I bought cookbooks, tried new cuisines, tested different vegetables, spices and techniques. I was on a mission!

At first, I cut out dairy and red meat from my diet because I kept reading articles stating that these two foods might exacerbate conditions like acne. I still ate white meat, fish and eggs for a while, but after a time I stopped eating meat altogether as I lost the taste for it. I also switched to delicious dairy substitutions, like unsweetened coconut yogurt instead of dairy yogurt and cashew cheese instead of regular cheese, plus I would attempt twists on classic dishes to give them a 'skin-friendly' spin and boost. And guess what? My skin finally started to clear. At that point I hadn't take any medication for almost 6 months, and although I was still getting breakouts they weren't as red and inflamed. For the first time in what felt like a lifetime, I finally had the wonderful feeling that I was on the right path to clearing my skin for good. I really couldn't believe that I had spent so many years going from doctor to doctor, looking for that miracle cure, when the answer had always been in front of me, right on my plate.

As well as meat and dairy, I also cut out refined sugar, fizzy drinks and processed confectionery products, which proved to be fundamental in clearing my skin. I was a bit of a sugar monster – that croissant for breakfast was just the tip of the iceberg. There was milk chocolate after lunch, biscuits with tea in the afternoon and chocolate mousse after dinner, to name just a few. Cutting out sugar was probably the hardest part for me, as I was definitely hooked. What really helped was when I started to create better-for-you sweet recipes, which would still satisfy my sweet tooth while also supporting my skin at the same time. Check out the Sweets chapter (page 162) to find out more!

These changes to my diet were revelatory. My digestion improved, my energy levels were higher, I no longer had that 4 p.m. slump, and I felt fitter and stronger than ever before. Eating a plant-based diet became second nature. I was coming up with so many scrumptious and satisfying recipes that I simply didn't feel the need to eat animal products anymore. My new wholefood diet felt very abundant and even lavish. I was no longer restricting my calories, counting them or controlling my portions. I was eating until I was full and satisfied, and my skin never looked better. I felt I had struck gold.

My boyfriend, friends and family were sceptical at the beginning and didn't think I was going to last long on this new lifestyle regime. When I told my mum, grandma and Italian family, I think it got the biggest laugh of the year. They found it almost insane that a girl from the home of ragù, tortellini, mortadella and so many other delights would want to turn her back on them. I still remember the horrified face of my boyfriend when I made my daily green smoothie, and as I crunched down a raw kale salad. But my family came around in the end, as they saw how determined I was and that it was making me confident and happy in my skin again.

As well as changing my diet, I implemented a few lifestyle changes. For the first time ever, I started to exercise consistently. By increasing blood flow, exercise helps to deliver oxygen and nutrients to the skin, which keeps it healthy and also promotes collagen and new skin cell production. Personally, I love a combination of HIIT workouts, low-impact weight training and Pilates. However, in a very similar way to diet, when it comes to exercise one size doesn't fit all. I would encourage you to find a type of movement that makes you feel good and that you enjoy, otherwise you will never stick to it for more than a week. It's also important to highlight that exercise that's too strenuous, or over-exercise in general, can negatively impact your hormones. This can lead to excess adrenaline and cortisol, which is something to be mindful of if you are trying to keep your skin blemish-free. Generally speaking, if you feel drained as opposed to energized after a workout, this might be a sign to switch things up. Also keep in mind that your body might feel different on different days. The workout that you love today may feel different next week. Always listen to your body, to its cues, and remember that you are exercising to feel better and to relieve stress, not to accumulate it. As the saying goes, sometimes less is more.

I also looked at my sleep schedule and stress levels. These two normally go hand in hand, as when we are under stress we tend to sleep poorly. Stress can increase the amount of oil your skin produces, which can clog pores and cause breakouts. On the other hand, getting restorative sleep is single-handedly one of the best things you can do for your skin (and it's free!). Sleep is one of those totally underrated beauty tools. Lack of sleep or poor-quality sleep can interfere with your food cravings (ever had a bad night's sleep and woken up craving a greasy or sugary breakfast?). It can alter your mood and even your levels of cortisol, the stress hormones that cause inflammation and can contribute to breakouts. As with exercise, during sleep your skin's blood flow increases, it rebuilds collagen and repairs damage from UVA exposure, reducing wrinkles and age spots. You might be eating all the kale in the world but if your quality of sleep is poor or you don't get enough of it, chances are it will show on your skin. My advice is to schedule 7 to 9 hours of sleep as you would schedule a meeting. Write in your diary what time you need to go to bed and stick to it – I promise you there is no Netflix show worth more than a rested and glowing complexion.

I saw first-hand the terrible effect that stress could have on my skin. For a short period of my life I was working in a stressful and toxic work environment. I was constantly frazzled, worried and busy and I was also eating badly and not sleeping properly, which just added more fuel to the flame! It was a vicious circle. As part of my overhaul, I started to look into mindfulness practices and meditation, which has helped me tremendously throughout the years to find peace and stillness when life gets chaotic.

The decision to change my diet and lifestyle was single-handedly the best thing I have ever done. It allowed me to take control of my health and finally clear my skin. I felt so inspired by the wonderful changes I was seeing in my health that I felt compelled to share the knowledge I had gathered with others. That's when my blog and Instagram account, Happy Skin Kitchen, was born. I never set out to do this full-time, let alone to write a book, but recipe after recipe my blog continued to grow and I realized that there were so many others going through the same problems as me. Now I am lucky enough to be able to do this for a living. Sharing healthy recipes with hundreds of thousands of people still feels so surreal, but the most incredible blessing at the same time!

Clearing my skin didn't happen overnight. It was a long and winding road with a lot of bumps along the way. It probably took me two years to finally have my clear skin back without the use of any medication. It wasn't an overnight miracle and the whole experience taught me that there is really no such thing as a quick fix, especially when it comes to skin health and health in general. I had to put in lots of time, love, patience and, most importantly, I had to commit to truly looking after myself in a more holistic and sustainable way. A way that will support my beauty and my health for many years to come.

I learned that what builds strong foundations for healthy skin is a nutritious daily diet, long-lasting lifestyle choices and a positive mindset. Real, tangible results come from consistent, ordinary, everyday actions that over time have the power to dramatically change how we look and feel, forever. They might seem insignificant at the beginning, for example I remember thinking: 'How is eating that extra handful of kale really going to make a difference?' but I promise you those tiny changes are the ones that, once you stack them together, snowball into being incredibly impactful. Those small habits will become the true foundation of your lifestyle and how you think about health and beauty for the rest of your life.

A New Way of Eating

All my recipes are vegan and gluten-free, but this book definitely doesn't set out to have an all or nothing approach. I know first-hand that eating a whole food plant-based diet can feel daunting. But my hope is that this book will show you that eating this way can be delicious, satisfying and a great way to support your beauty from the inside out. It can be so easy to try to fix your skin from the outside by slapping on an array of topical products, but the first step to healthy, radiant skin starts with what you put inside your body and therefore what's on your plate.

In all honesty, the negative impact that animal agriculture has on the environment wasn't really at the forefront of my mind. However, with the talk in recent years of the climate emergency we are now facing, with Greta doing her thing and the fact that one of the easiest ways to make a positive impact is by consuming fewer animal products, it provided even more incentive to join the plant-based revolution. Do you have to be fully vegan to be more environment-friendly? I don't think you do – you can still have a positive impact on the planet by switching to a flexitarian diet (a diet mostly centred around plant-based foods but with room for animal products every so often), which I think is a very doable and less intimidating solution and something everyone can start doing right now.

I apply the same approach when it comes to looking after my skin. The Happy Skin Kitchen philosophy is all about embracing (and enjoying!) a plant-centred diet with an abundance of colourful fruits, vegetables, legumes, nuts and seeds. This approach will ensure plenty of vitamins, minerals and other compounds such as phytochemicals, essential for glowing skin, strong nails and luscious healthy hair. If you have the desire to add some animal products to this approach, then by all means listen to your body and go for it!

When it comes to creating my recipes I love celebrating everyday ingredients, like the humble broccoli, sweet potato and cauliflower, by elevating them into something surprisingly delicious that will also make your skin sing with joy. Maybe it's because I am Italian, but aside from eating for nourishment and fuel, I eat for the sheer pleasure of it. I tend to gravitate towards abundance in my recipes, in colours (more colours = a wider range of antioxidants for glowing skin!), textures and flavours aimed to please plant eaters and omnivores alike.

One of the most common myths about a healthy plant-based diet is that it is expensive, perhaps because we tend to associate it with superfoods, protein powders and other fancy, hard-to-get ingredients which can be off-putting and totally out of reach for some. However, I firmly believe that cooking wholesome and nutritious plant-based meals doesn't have to break the bank, especially when you are focusing on simple everyday ingredients. For example, beef and chicken can cost about four times as much as dried lentils. It's all about focusing on hero staples like beans, lentils, wholegrains and seasonal produce, and making them a big part of your shopping list.

The bottom line is that I am not here to tell anyone exactly how to eat and what not to eat. The only person who can decide that is you. I am here to equip you with knowledge, tips and ideas, which can help you to make better choices when it comes to feeding and nourishing your skin. This book is flexible and adaptable. I love eating a 100 per cent plant-based diet but that doesn't mean you have to do the same. I believe you can still reap some incredible benefits eating like this 80 per cent of the time. I would encourage you to find what works for you, your body and your skin, and more importantly, find a balance that makes healthy eating sustainable and enjoyable in the long term. My hope is to inspire you to think more about the food you eat and what it can do for your skin, with recipes and beauty rituals that can be easily incorporated into your existing routine. The book can be used as a starting point to suit your own lifestyle.

A NOTE ON GLUTEN

I've kept all my recipes gluten-free to make them accessible for as many people as possible, and listening to my community's feedback gluten intolerances and sensitivities are very common. I personally don't have any issues with gluten and my skin seems to be OK with it, too. If you don't have any issues with gluten there is really no reason why you should avoid it completely. My advice would be to focus on whole unrefined grains, as they offer a 'complete package' of health benefits, unlike refined grains which are stripped of valuable nutrients in the refining process.

> "The first step to healthy, radiant skin starts with what you put inside your body and therefore what's on your plate."

Even if you are not gluten free I would recommend that you stick with the flours and ingredients I use, especially in the Sweets chapter, not only because the recipes have been tried and tested so are guaranteed to work, but because all the flours and ingredients I've used are also designed to nourish your skin with every bite.

A NOTE ON ORGANIC

My dad has been growing his own organic fruit and veg for over 30 years and I have seen first-hand how much harder it is to grow produce without the use of conventional pesticides. Because of that I have a huge respect and appreciation for organic farming, which is also kinder to the environment and wildlife. From a health and skin perspective, there are studies which have shown that the use of pesticides might increase the amount of free radicals in the body and affect hormonal balance. However, buying organic produce can be considerably more expensive and is not accessible for everyone, so my advice would be if you can afford it and it fits with your values go forth, otherwise don't sweat it. Non-organic wholefoods like fruit, vegetables, wholegrains, legumes, nuts and seeds are still all incredibly nutrient-dense and crucial for our skin health and longevity.

PLANT MILKS

Although plant milks are fashionable these days, which is great from a planetary perspective, they are not all created equal. Lots of them contain added sugar, emulsifiers and other not-so-skin-friendly additives. Fortunately, there are healthier plant-based milk brands that are unsweetened and contain fewer ingredients. Look for brands that have only the nut (almond, cashew, coconut) or the grain (oat, rice), plus simple ingredients like filtered water and sea salt.

The Skin &
Gut Connection

Over the last decade or so we have heard more and more about the importance of a good gut for our all-round health. There is a lot of research behind this, and the buzz word is 'gut microbiome'. Your gut microbiome consists of trillions of micro-organisms that live in your gut and bring all sorts of different skills to the party. First and foremost it aids digestion and works hard to extract all the nutrients from food and drinks we consume, but it also helps with the production of certain vitamins and essential amino acids that support immunity, brain function and – you guessed it – improve skin health.

The skin partners with the gut and plays a vital role in expelling toxins, waste and other nasties. In fact, our skin often tells us exactly what is going on in our body and gives us warning signs. If your skin is irritated, inflamed or congested, it may be that you have some kind of imbalance in your gut. I experienced this first-hand when, after a 6-month course of antibiotics to clear my skin, I found my digestion was completely out of whack and as a result, my skin was more inflamed and irritated than ever before.

There is heaps we can do to nurture and support our gut microbiome through positive diet and lifestyle decisions. I look at my gut like a garden. If I tend to it with care and love, it will reward me with a diverse range of flowers and plants – aka a wide range of beneficial bacteria that live in symbiosis and balance. By ensuring that we have a good balance of bacteria, our internal ecosystem will thrive.

How to Take Care of Your Gut for Glowing Skin

1. MOSTLY PLANTS

There is no question that fibre-rich plants are our gut microbiome's favourite food, so make sure to get a selection of vegetables, beans, wholegrains, nuts and seeds daily.

2. FOCUS ON DIVERSITY

Our diverse set of microbes love different plant-based foods. Try to aim for 30 different plants every week.

3. WHOLEFOODS OVER PROCESSED

When you eat wholefoods you get more fibre, more vitamins, minerals and overall more nutrition – it's really a no-brainer!

4. LOVE YOUR PULSES

In my opinion they are one of the most underrated foods on the planet. Beans, chickpeas and lentils are loaded with fibre and they are one of the most cost-efficient, versatile, nutrient-dense foods.

5. GET FERMENTING

This is one of the simplest and most effective ways to support gut health and wellbeing. Check out my fermented foods chapter (page 252) to find out more.

6. PAUSE AND CHEW

Make the time to sit down at the dinner table and avoid eating on the go. Digestion begins in the mouth, so chewing properly helps to trigger the release of digestive enzymes and increases the surface area of the food, allowing the enzymes to act more efficiently.

How Food Makes You Beautiful

As I write this book, the beauty industry in the UK alone is worth a staggering £2.7 billion. Don't get me wrong, I'm not a hater – I absolutely love my skincare routine! I religiously apply my SPF every morning and cleanse my face at night, followed by my beloved retinol serum and my night cream. Having a solid skincare routine is important, but when we match it with a beauty-supporting diet, rich in minerals, antioxidants and vitamins, that's when the magic happens. When I eat poorly, even now, it shows clearly on my skin. My skin tends to break out, it becomes drier, my fine lines are more enhanced and I have a greyish kind of complexion. Definitely far from healthy and glowing! We overlook and underestimate the power of foods and the clear link between beauty and nutrition, placing too much emphasis on outside fixes. We pay £50 for a special serum and spend hours pampering, but we'll skimp on paying a few pounds for some quality ingredients and go for the easy takeaway option instead. I was definitely guilty of that, and for the longest time I completely disregarded my diet and just focused on finding the next 'miracle product'. Of course genetics plays a role and ageing is unavoidable and completely natural, but when you eat a healthy, anti-ageing beauty diet you give your skin the best chance to glow and look youthful well into your 40s, 50s and beyond.

What Makes a Beauty Food?

It's time to look at food as your most powerful beauty tool! Think about this: the food you consume becomes your body on a molecular level. This is one of the most significant reasons that the quality of your diet is so important to your skin. Every breakfast, lunch and dinner doesn't just enter and exit your body, those nutrients stick around and become the building blocks of your skin, hair and nails. Would you choose to build your body and your skin using the best, most nutrient-dense material or would you opt for low-quality, nutritionally poor foods?

When it comes to looking and feeling your best, focus on foods loaded with skin heroes to nourish your beauty from inside out. The 4 main attributes to look for are:

1 RICH IN MICRONUTRIENTS: beauty-enhancing vitamins, minerals, antioxidants and phytochemicals.

2 NUTRIENT-DENSE: rich in nutrients – including high-quality protein, complex carbohydrates and good fats.

3 UNREFINED: as little processing as possible, to maintain the most nutritional value.

4 HIGH-FIBRE: to feed our gut bacteria, slow digestion and promote satiety and regular elimination.

1. Rich in Micronutrients

An optimal skin diet includes essential vitamins, minerals and antioxidants. These combat free radicals and compounds formed in our day-to-day life, from activities such as sun exposure, air pollution, stress, exercise, smoking and more. Free radicals cause damage – not only to our skin but also inside our bodies. Antioxidants are the superheroes that take free radicals out of circulation by supplying them with the electrons they are seeking, without doing any harm to the body. The more antioxidants we consume, the greater protection we have against the effects of ageing.

Listing all the beauty vitamins and minerals is an almost impossible task, but these are some of my favourites, which you will find in abundance in my recipes. They have the power to supercharge your beauty and your health too.

VITAMIN C: Essential for collagen production. Collagen is a protein fibre that gives your skin strength and keeps it firm. As you age, the production of collagen reduces naturally. Vitamin C is also a powerful antioxidant and plays a part in protecting the skin from free radicals.

Where to find it: Red peppers, strawberries, kale, cabbage, kiwis and citrus fruit.

VITAMIN A: Fights free radicals, promotes the growth of healthy new skin cells and strengthens the skin. Vitamin A also helps to regulate sebum production, aka fewer breakouts.

Where to find it: Sweet potatoes, butternut squash, pumpkins, carrots, kale, collard greens and spinach.

VITAMIN E: Another free radical fighter, this fat-soluble vitamin is secreted via your sebum to help protect the surface of your skin and prevent inflammation.

Where to find it: Avocados, almonds, sunflower seeds, olives and extra virgin olive oil, tomatoes and spinach.

VITAMIN B7 (BIOTIN): Helps to protect your skin cells from water loss, among other things. If you find yourself with dry skin, brittle nails or scaly scalp, it might be a sign you are not getting enough.

Where to find it: Legumes, wholegrains, almonds, avocados, walnuts and nutritional yeast.

VITAMIN B3 (NIACIN): Helps to keep your skin soft, healthy and glowing and is also essential for DNA repair.

Where to find it: Collard greens, kale, mushrooms, avocados, sunflower seeds and peas.

VITAMIN B5 (PANTHOTHENIC ACID): Supports new skin cell growth and helps maintain skin moisture. It also helps to regulate the production of cortisol, your stress hormone, which is important for a blemish-free complexion.

Where to find it: Wholegrains, broccoli, mushrooms, avocados and sweet potatoes.

ZINC: One of the most important healing minerals for skin health, and particularly important for acne-prone skin. Zinc controls the production of oil in the skin and helps control some of the hormones that can cause acne.

Where to find it: Pumpkin seeds, cashews, walnuts, legumes, chia seeds, quinoa and tahini.

"We underestimate the power of foods and the clear link between beauty and nutrition, placing too much emphasis on outside fixes."

COPPER: A great skin ally, promoting the production of collagen and elastin which give the skin its strength and elasticity. Copper also helps to enhance the function of antioxidants, which in turn help to protect the skin from oxidative damage.

Where to find it: Kale, collard greens, sunflower seeds, hazelnuts, walnuts, cashews, pecans and mushrooms.

SELENIUM: Another important mineral for skin health, a strong antioxidant that's essential for maintaining skin elasticity and flexibility.

Where to find it: Brazil nuts, mushrooms and oats.

MAGNESIUM: Crucial mineral for skin health, bones, teeth, hair and the muscles, and it helps keep the nervous system running smoothly. A magnesium deficiency can potentially accelerate ageing of the skin.

Where to find it: Black beans, kale, collard greens, cashews, pumpkin seeds, quinoa and oats.

CALCIUM: I guess we all know the importance of calcium intake for healthy teeth and bones, but it's also an essential mineral for skin health, playing a major role in providing firmness and elasticity to the skin as well as to all tissues and cells of the body.

Where to find it: Tahini, tofu, tempeh, broccoli, kale, collard greens, almonds, hazelnuts and chickpeas.

SILICA: A trace mineral that helps strengthen your body's connective tissues – muscles, tendons, hair, ligaments, nails, cartilage and bone – and a vital component in maintaining healthy skin.

Where to find it: Bananas, brown rice, oats, cucumbers, red cabbage, beans and chickpeas.

2. Nutrient-dense

There are three fundamental macronutrients to keep in mind when building your Happy Skin plate. I look at these as building blocks to base most of my meals around.

PROTEIN FOR YOUTHFUL SKIN

Protein is the main structural component of our bodies and an important beauty nutrient. Hair, nails, muscles and all cells in the body need a constant supply of protein to grow, repair and basically do their job. Protein is also an essential component of collagen, the connective tissue that provides support for glowing skin. You don't need to be a meat-eater to get plenty of protein in your diet: some of my favourite sources of protein are beans and lentils, hemp seeds, tempeh and tofu. The added bonus of choosing protein derived from plants is that they are naturally high in fibre (apart from tofu), which is important for our gut health. Varying the different plant-based proteins is the best way to get a well-rounded supply of amino acids, the molecules that make up the protein.

CARBOHYDRATES FOR SUSTAINED ENERGY

Carbohydrates are not the villains they are often portrayed to be. They can provide beauty nutrients and glucose, which is converted to energy and acts as the primary source of fuel for our brain and muscles. Carbohydrates are not all created equal, and there is a huge difference between refined and ultra-processed carbs, like white bread, cereals and biscuits, and complex carbohydrates like starchy vegetables, wholegrains and legumes. This latter group is the one to focus on, as these are rich in vitamins, minerals, antioxidants and fibre.

FATS FOR SUPPLE SKIN

I am so glad that the low-fat/fat-free craze seems to be officially a thing of the past. Today we know that healthy fats supply certain essential fatty acids that your body can't make but that are key to supple skin. Fats also allow your body to absorb fat-soluble vitamins that are essential for skin health, such as vitamins A, D, E and K. Not all fats are the same: simply put, there are bad fats that we should try to avoid or limit as much as possible, and good fats that will support beneficial body processes. The type of good fats you should focus on are monounsaturated and polyunsaturated. In the plant world you find these in avocados, nuts and seeds, olives and extra virgin olive oil. The bad fats you should try to avoid are the saturated fats, which are usually found in ultra-processed foods, fast foods, red meat, butter and cheese.

3. Unrefined

Unrefined foods are those which have been minimally processed from their natural state. When we eat unrefined foods we get the 'whole package' that Mother Nature intended for us. Whole foods are rich in vital vitamins, minerals, antioxidants and fibre. All of these elements play an essential role in our overall health and are fundamental building blocks for beauty, too.

Examples of unrefined foods include fruits, vegetables, nuts, seeds, legumes and whole grains. Refined foods include white flours, white sugar, margarine and confectionery products such as biscuits, sweets and crackers. These foods have been processed so much that the beneficial fibre, vitamins and minerals have been removed, leaving very little nutritional value that our body can utilise.

I look at whole, unrefined foods as the ultimate skin foods. By filling up your plate with these nutrient-dense foods you are supporting your body and skin for many years to come.

4. High-fibre

One of the simplest and most efficient ways to support our gut is to make sure we feed it with its favourite food, fibre. Fibre is only found in plant-based foods and the current guidelines say most adults should be aiming for 30g of fibre each day. To give you an example, 1 cup of cooked chickpeas gives you about 12.5g of dietary fibre, 1 cup of oats gives 8g, and 1 cup of quinoa gives you about 5g of fibre. You can see how quickly things add up, and how easy it can be to get plenty of fibre in a wholefood, plant-based diet. Another important factor to take into consideration is variety. Each plant food has its own mix of different types of fibre that feed unique sets of microbes housed in the gut. This allows our microbes not only to grow, but to thrive. For optimal gut health, we should aim for 30 different plant-based foods each week. At first, I thought that there was no way I could get so many different plants into my diet each week, so I made a list and it was interesting to see how easy it actually is. Try things like adding a sprinkle of nuts and seeds to your avocado toast, adding a handful of chopped kale to your pasta, adding extra veggies to a soup, or fortifying stews with lentils or beans.

My Top 15 Skingredients

My top 15 Skingredients are packed with powerful nutrients and micro-nutrients to support and feed your skin from within. It's quite hard to come up with a definitive list of foods that are best for beauty as there are so many – however, some foods definitely pack more of a punch than others, so here are 15 of my favourites, and why including them in your diet can help you achieve your beauty goals. They are the building blocks of so many of the recipes you will find in this book and are utterly delicious when used and cooked in the right way. Be ready to eat yourself beautiful!

1. KALE
Risen in popularity in the past few years for all the right reasons, since it's one of the most nutrient-dense foods on the planet. Even just 1 cup of kale would exceed your recommended daily amount of both vitamin C and vitamin A. Vitamin C is essential for boosting collagen production (hence its presence in so many beauty products), and vitamin A is a powerful skin smoother because it boosts cell turnover. Kale also supports detoxification in the liver, important for clear skin, and contains the phytochemicals lutein and zeaxanthin, shown to help protect eyes from ageing. Kale was probably the one vegetable I really struggled with at first because of its bitterness and sturdy leaves, but once I learned how to cook it properly it became a regular staple in my diet. Check out my Kale, Apple & Fennel Salad (page 174) for some delicious inspiration.

2. SWEET POTATOES
Full of beta-carotene, an antioxidant pigment that converts in the body to the powerful beauty of vitamin A. Sweet potatoes are also rich in vitamin C and vitamin E. This complex carb is guaranteed to

keep you satisfied for longer, which is why I often eat sweet potatoes at lunchtime to keep me feeling full until dinner. Check out my Warm Sweet Potato Noodle Salad (page 171) for a quick lunch idea.

3. BROCCOLI

An excellent source of wrinkle-preventing vitamin C, bone-reinforcing calcium, potassium and vitamin K to help strengthen capillaries and prevent dark circles. All this, plus it contains the phytochemical sulforaphane, which helps prevent stress-related inflammation. Sadly, broccoli always tends to be considered a side veg, but in my opinion it is highly overlooked. Fall in love with broccoli again with my Chilli Broccoli Salad (page 182).

4. BEETROOT

Contain collagen-building vitamin C, iron, beta-carotene and vitamin K to defend against bruising and support healthy bones. They also contain lycopene, a plant chemical that helps maintain youthful skin elasticity and can even help to protect the skin from sun damage. Even if you are not a beet lover, you have to try my Balsamic Beetroot with Whipped Tahini Cream (page 168) or my Purple Beet Kraut (page 260) – I promise you won't regret it!

5. WALNUTS

An amazing plant source of skin-strengthening omega-3 fatty acids, converted from alpha-linolenic acid. These healthy fats may also reduce skin inflammation (aka fewer breakouts) and play a role in protecting the skin against harmful UV rays. Walnuts are also full of other important minerals, such as zinc for healthy skin and scalp. I absolutely love the versatility of walnuts in cooking, from pesto and salads, to crumbles and granolas. Check out my Cheesy Walnut & Hemp Parm (page 106) for a super-nutritious boost to a meal.

6. HEMP SEEDS

These tiny but mighty seeds are a complete source of protein that supports cell building and repair for healthy skin, nails and hair. They are also an excellent source of anti-ageing and anti-inflammatory omega-3 fatty acids. Hemp seeds are rich in fibre, which helps to maintain a healthy gut, as well as in iron and zinc. I love sprinkling hemp seeds on pretty much anything – they have a really mild flavour. From porridge, rye toast, baked potatoes, to salads and soups, this wonder seed is an easy beauty boost to any meal. Check out my Raw Brownie Protein Bars (page 222) for a decadent and protein-packed snack.

7. ALMONDS

An excellent source of vitamin E, that precious beauty vitamin that keeps your skin moisturized and protected from the sun. Plus they are also a great plant-based source of calcium, copper and magnesium. Not only are almonds delicious, they are so versatile too! I love using them ground in baking, chopped up in salads and buddha bowls and check out my Chickpea and Almond Curry (page 139) for a creamy savoury dish.

8. PUMPKIN SEEDS

One of the best plant-based sources of zinc, an essential anti-inflammatory mineral that encourages clear skin as well as hair growth and strong nails. Pumpkin seeds also contain a long list of anti-ageing nutrients, like omega-3s and vitamins A, B and K, as well as minerals like niacin, magnesium, copper and iron. I love to add a sprinkle of pumpkin seeds to my breakfast porridge, salads and buddha bowls – and if you want an extra delicious way of using this mighty seed, check out my Roasted Tamari Super-seed Mix (page 107).

9. CHICKPEAS

Antioxidant-rich and full of zinc, which is an important nutrient for immune function. Chickpeas are also rich in protein, fibre and folate. They are affordable, available pretty much everywhere and make a great base for so many recipes. I love them in my Caponata Chickpea Pasta (page 112), but they are also great in sweet recipes like my Double Chocolate Cookie Dough Bars (page 276). I know that might sound a bit odd, but trust me, they are surprisingly delicious!

10. AVOCADO

Nothing beats a perfectly ripe, creamy, buttery avocado! I call it nature's most indulgent gift, and it's also one of the most beautifying fats, keeping your skin dewy and soft. Avocados are rich in vitamin E, which helps your skin cells stay strong and hydrated, and in B vitamins like niacin that assist in detox, DNA repair and reducing redness and inflammation in the skin. Try my Spring Picnic Salad with avocado mayo dressing (page 176) and fall in love with this wonder fruit even more.

11. BERRIES

Absolutely loaded with antioxidants, berries contain the highest amount of any fruit, with pomegranates next on the list. Berries are also rich in vitamin C – for example, just 1 cup of strawberries contains a whopping 150 per cent of the recommended daily intake! I absolutely love berries and refer to them as nature's sweets.

They are sweet, delicious and they make a great topping for any porridge, bircher muesli or chia pudding. Check out my Strawberry & Cream Bircher Muesli (page 62) for a decadent breakfast on the go.

12. CHIA SEEDS

Another tiny but mighty seed packed to the brim with skin goodies. Chia seeds have high levels of antioxidants, which we know fight free radicals, and are also rich in omega-3 fatty acids that strengthen the skin barrier and keep it protected from environmental harm. Furthermore they are high in nutrients such as vitamin A, vitamin C, iron and potassium, which can help boost skin luminosity and elasticity. Make my Coconut & Vanilla Chia Pudding with Berry Compote (page 214) for a nourishing dessert.

13. LENTILS

Totally underrated and often overlooked, lentils have a substantial protein content and are great for sustained energy and stable blood sugar levels. They are also rich in folate, which is essential for DNA synthesis and cell repair, as well as iron, for strong nails. I love lentils because they are quick to cook – try my Moroccan-inspired Lentil & Carrot Soup (page 150) for a super-easy dinner idea.

14. MUSHROOMS

With antioxidant and anti-inflammatory properties, mushrooms contain two specific antioxidants (ergothioneine and glutathione) that help protect against free-radical damage. I particularly love shiitake mushrooms – they are rich in selenium, which can decrease irritation and calm inflammation, keeping your skin happy and supple. But even the humble white button mushroom is chock-full of nutrients such as the B vitamins that help protect our skin's elasticity. Check out my Almond Butter & Shiitake Mushroom Bowl (page 85) for a brilliant fuss-free dinner.

15. GARLIC

Rich in compounds such as allicin, sulphur, zinc and calcium, which have health and beauty benefits as well as antibiotic and antifungal properties. Allicin, in particular, helps kill the bacteria that cause acne. It also helps to reduce swelling and inflammation and improves blood circulation. Garlic is a firm staple in my kitchen. Not only does it have incredible health and skin benefits but it's a very inexpensive way to add a lot of flavour. My Harissa Sweet Potatoes with Roasted Garlic & Tahini Dressing (page 235) is a great crowd-pleaser recipe that's perfect for entertaining.

Happy Skin Kitchen Pantry Staples

As you go through the book you will see that the same ingredients crop up time and again. This is intentional, as I don't want you to buy millions of different ingredients that you will use only once or twice. I am hoping to show you that once you have plenty of fresh produce in the fridge and a fairly well-stocked pantry, making healthy and nourishing meals is easy and not too time-consuming. I started eating this way when I was still in my fast-paced fashion job, so there was no way I was able to spend hours in the kitchen every day. The key when it comes to eating healthily is to get organized, especially if you have a busy schedule. I know this sounds a bit boring, but if your cupboards are stocked with everything you need to make a nourishing meal, you are more likely to actually make it rather than ordering a takeaway.

When it comes to pantry staples, I find it easy to just order everything online every couple of months, as it saves me carrying heavy bags from store to store. These are some of my favourites, which you will encounter in many of the recipes. They are all wonderful building blocks for delicious and easy meals, and they pack a nutritional punch too.

BUCKWHEAT AND BUCKWHEAT FLOUR

Despite the name, buckwheat has nothing to do with wheat and is actually a seed, not a grain, so it's naturally gluten-free. Buckwheat has an excellent nutritional profile: it's high in fibre, protein, calcium and magnesium, and it's also rich in antioxidants like rutin, which helps protect the skin from sun damage. Buckwheat flour is probably my favourite gluten-free flour, as it has a delicious nutty flavour and works well in so many baking recipes, like my Lemon & Coconut Loaf (page 269) or my Apple & Raisin Loaf (page 282).

OATS

Incredibly nutritious, high in fibre and loaded with vitamins, minerals and antioxidants. Oats are particularly high in the soluble fibre beta-glucan, which has numerous benefits; it helps reduce cholesterol and blood sugar levels, promotes healthy gut bacteria and increases feelings of fullness. One exceptional skin-loving antioxidant found in large amounts in oats is ferulic acid. You might have seen it listed in lots of skincare products, as it helps to protect skin integrity by reducing the development of fine lines, spots and wrinkles. I love oats because they are affordable and so versatile. I like using them in my bircher muesli, granola and porridge, but they are also an excellent baking staple and you'll find them in my Muesli Muffins (page 274) and Fruity Flapjacks (page 210), perfect for a mid-afternoon pick me up.

QUINOA

One of my favourite pseudo-grains, although it's technically a seed. Quinoa has a low glycemic index, is a complete source of protein, meaning it has all the 9 essential amino acids, is high in iron and is brimming with antioxidants. Quinoa is also rich in B vitamin nutrients that help treat age spots and other conditions related to skin pigmentation by reducing the deposits of dark melanin in the skin. I love it because it's really quick to cook and it's a great protein addition to virtually any meal. It's amazing in porridge and baking, especially in my Nutrient-dense Bread (page 226).

WHOLEGRAIN PASTA

Pasta to Italians is what potatoes are to the British – well, certainly to my fiancé. While he has been brought up on spuds cooked in numerous ways, pasta has been the centre of my food universe since I was a bambina. There is no question that it is my number-one favourite food, and I really don't understand why it always seems to get a bad rep, especially when there are now so many wholesome types of pasta that are higher in fibre and protein. In the gluten-free world, my favourite is brown rice pasta – I find it holds its shape like regular wheat pasta and is much easier and lighter to digest. I also love chickpea pasta for its higher protein content. If you are not gluten-free, try wholemeal spelt pasta which is another favourite of mine as it's high in fibre and has a delicious nutty flavour. One of the many reasons why I love pasta is that it is the ultimate fast food and you can pack so much goodness into a single bowl. For a speedy dinner, I simply sauté some onion and garlic in olive oil, chop and throw in whatever veg I have in the fridge along with some herbs and a tin of chopped tomatoes. Then I cook everything together along with my pasta of choice and in less than 15 minutes I have a healthy

and delicious meal. For a speedy and veggie-fuelled lunch, try my Pea & Broccoli Pasta (page 114), which comes together in just over 20 minutes.

COCONUT MILK

I just love how creamy and decadent coconut milk is. It's naturally sweet, with that gorgeous nutty flavour that instantly makes me dream of lazy days at the beach. I mostly use it in curries and dhals, such as my Black Dhal (page 136) or my Dhal Pita (page 124), making them extra rich and flavoursome, but it's also great in porridge and smoothies.

NUTRITIONAL YEAST

This is a deactivated yeast. It has a nutty, cheesy and savoury flavour and is usually used in vegan cooking to recreate cheesy sauces, vegan cheeses and cheesy casseroles. It's the key ingredient in my Cheesy Walnut & Hemp Parm (page 106), which takes 2 minutes to make, and it really adds tons of flavour to any Happy Skin bowl or pasta dish. Nutritional yeast is also a great source of protein, vitamins and minerals, making it a nutritious and versatile ingredient in dairy-free dishes. People are generally a bit sceptical about nutritional yeast – I totally appreciate that it sounds and smells a bit weird but trust me, once you start using it you will not be able to live without it.

NUT BUTTERS

I am totally addicted to nut butters. You will often find me eating them straight from the jar. A spoonful of nut butter is a great addition to any smoothie or porridge as it adds a deliciously rich texture, a flavour boost and lots of healthy fats, protein and minerals. I love to dip a sliced of apple into almond butter as a quick afternoon snack, and I add peanut butter to my smoothies to keep me fuller for longer. Nut butters are also great for adding creaminess to salad dressings, such as the almond butter dressing for my Sunshine Slaw (page 178).

TINNED TOMATOES

I know tinned tomatoes might not sound that exciting, but cooked tomatoes are a wonderful source of the skin-loving antioxidant lycopene, which protects the skin against sun exposure. Tinned tomatoes are super-handy when you need to quickly rustle up a meal and you don't have much food in the house. Alongside onion and garlic you have a perfect pasta sauce, and with a few spices and vegetables added they can be the basis of an array of stews, curries and casseroles. Just check the ingredients before you buy them to make sure they have no added preservatives or sugars.

TINNED BEANS AND PULSES

Legumes are a fundamental part of a wholefood plant-based diet, as they are a powerhouse of minerals, vitamins, fibre and of course protein. In an ideal world we would all cook our beans from scratch, but the reality is that most of us won't be able to find the time or will forget to do it. Hence, tinned ready-cooked beans are a wonderful staple for creating nourishing and filling meals in minutes (buy BPA free tins if you can – my favourite brands are Biona and Mr Organic). I always have several tins of beans in my storecupboard so all I have to do is open the tin, drain the liquid, and I am good to go. I love to use pulses in stews and soups, but they are also great in dips and even smoothies! Check out my Chickpea Chocolate Smoothie (page 191).

EXTRA VIRGIN OLIVE OIL

It may be because I'm Italian but there are few things that make me happier than a bottle of good quality extra virgin olive oil. It might seem like an unnecessary indulgence, but trust me – spending some extra pennies on the highest quality olive oil you can afford is so worth it! Good olive oil has a strong and fruity flavour, which will make the biggest difference in your salad dressings or even if you simply drizzle it over a tray of roasted vegetables. Extra virgin olive oil is also a great source of vitamin E, which protects the skin from oxidative stress and provides a good dose of healthy monounsaturated fats.

APPLE CIDER VINEGAR

I use apple cider vinegar in most of my salad dressings, as it's a great way to add a tangy twist and lots of goodness too. Apple cider vinegar is made by a fermentation process, meaning it contains living probiotics which are important for feeding our gut microbiome. To take advantage of its incredible health benefits, make sure you buy unpasteurized or 'with the mother' apple cider vinegar, as it means all the goodness will still be in the bottle.

TAMARI SAUCE

A Japanese version of soy sauce, the main difference being that tamari contains no wheat, making it suitable for gluten-free diets. I use tamari in dressings, Asian-inspired dishes such as my Kimchi Noodle Soup (page 156), and even in simple stews or tomato sauces to add punch. Tamari has a rich umami flavour, so it can really make a difference when seasoning your food, giving every dish extra depth.

MISO PASTE

Miso is a fermented soybean paste. Similar to tamari, it has a very rich, umami flavour that can really complement savoury dishes. There are lots of different types of miso on the market. I usually buy red or brown miso paste, as I find these more affordable and widely available. Like tamari, miso paste is great in dressings but I also often add a tablespoon to lentil- or legume-based dishes like my Creamy Cannellini, Mushroom & Cavolo Nero Stew (page 159).

TAHINI

A sesame seed paste, and it's safe to say I am slightly obsessed with it. I use it in hummus, in dressings and sometimes I will just dip a square of dark chocolate into my tahini jar for a bit of pure heaven (don't mock it until you try it!). Tahini is rich in minerals such as calcium and zinc, which help keep breakouts at bay, and in omega-3 fatty acids, which help to moisturize the skin and reduce inflammation. If you've tried tahini in the past and it was bitter and grainy, then I am afraid that wasn't authentic tahini. Real tahini should be completely silky smooth and pourable. The best places to buy good quality tahini are Middle Eastern and Turkish food stores. If you don't have one of these in your area, the brand Belazu does a pretty good one.

SPICES

The heart and soul of any kitchen and the easiest and healthiest way to inject lots of flavour into any recipe. They can transform a pretty bland dish into something dazzling and delectable. They are also jam-packed with skin-loving antioxidants, so you get an incredible boost of flavour plus all the nutrition too! My favourites are: cinnamon, which has antibacterial and blood glucose stabilizing properties, so it's great for clear and glowing skin; cumin, which is rich in antimicrobial and anti-inflammatory properties, which help to soothe the skin and keep it free from blemishes; turmeric, which is brimming with antioxidants and is highly anti-inflammatory, ideal for blemish-prone skin and to help slow down ageing. Even just a handful of spices in your cupboard can help add layers of flavour to even the simplest dishes.

Beauty Betrayers

We are all individuals with different needs, and what works for one person might not necessarily work for another. I don't believe in an 'all or nothing' approach, or in anything that feels too restrictive or depriving. I know the word balance has been thrown around a lot lately, but in order to look after your skin and your body in the long term, try to find a lifestyle which is sustainable and doesn't feel like you are constantly on 'a diet'. I eat a wholesome plant-based diet 80 to 90 per cent of the time, but that doesn't mean I don't splurge every once in a while with some vegan junk food or takeaway. In the past, I went through a phase when I would obsess about eating 'clean' (whatever that even means) all the time. I think I was just so terrified that my spots were going to reappear if I deviated from eating healthily all the time. It almost became a life-consuming mission. It was also at the time when clean eating was ramping up on social media, and if you weren't sugar-free, gluten-free, oil-free or something-free, then you weren't doing it well enough. Long story short, I was only able to sustain such a restrictive diet for about two or three weeks. By the end of it, I was pretty miserable (with no social life), and I remember going to Crosstown (my favourite doughnut joint in London) and having the biggest doughnut I could get my hands on, and then of course feeling guilty about it straight away. I knew I would never be able to sustain such a restrictive diet for the rest of my life. I had to find a balance between a way of eating that nourished and fed my skin and a way of living that was also fun, sociable and enjoyable. I am so happy to have found a middle ground where I eat a healthy and wholesome diet the majority of the time but still leave room for spontaneity. Sometimes it might be a greasy (vegan) burger out with friends, an ice cream on holiday or a packet of crisps at a bar. The point is that I always enjoy every bite without any guilt attached. Life is too short to feel guilty about food, and what we eat occasionally doesn't affect our skin health in the long run. What matters is what we eat the majority of the time.

Of course, there are certain foods that are not great for our skin, and if you find yourself suffering from severe skin conditions like acne, rosacea or eczema these are foods and drinks that you certainly want to be mindful of avoiding. I am not saying that they should never ever grace your plate, but it's important to relegate them to an occasional treat, rather than a daily or weekly habit.

ALCOHOL

Don't get me wrong, it's fun to have a celebratory drink once in a while, but since I learned the devastating effect that alcohol has on the skin, it really has lost its appeal. Drinking alcohol results in two things: dehydration and inflammation. It dehydrates the skin, depriving it of the moisture and nutrients it needs to keep our complexion looking radiant and supple. The result is sagginess, dullness and premature ageing. Alcohol consumption is also a culprit for giving inflammatory signals within the skin, causing redness and flushing due to its vasodilatory effect. This can result in redness, blotchiness and puffiness. And if you are suffering from skin conditions like acne and rosacea, it's very likely that alcohol will exacerbate your symptoms.

REFINED SUGAR

It's just bad news for your skin. If you consume too much, it damages the collagen and elastin in your skin, making it look dull and more prone to wrinkles. Our body's collagen production naturally slows down from our mid-twenties and eating too much sugar just accelerates the process.

"Life is too short to feel guilty about food, and what we eat occasionally doesn't affect our skin health in the long run. What matters is what we eat the majority of the time."

ULTRA-PROCESSED FOODS

These are low in skin nutrition (and nutrition in general) and high in preservatives, chemical additives and artificial colourings and flavourings. These kinds of foods provoke early signs of ageing inflammation and lead to the production of free radicals. Ultra-processed foods are also usually high in unhealthy saturated fats and even in trans fats, which stimulate oil production in the skin, leading to clogged pores and more breakouts. Many processed foods are also high in added sugars which damage the collagen and elastin in your skin. Finally, many processed foods contain too much salt, which can be dehydrating, causing fine lines and wrinkles to show up more. I look at processed foods as 'silent thieves', in the sense that they might seem super-convenient but they actually rob you of valuable nutrition. For example, if you choose to eat a microwaveable meal and some chips for dinner you are missing out on the real nutrients that you could be getting if you were eating a home-made chickpea and veggie curry with a side of brown rice and kale instead. We are so accustomed to convenience foods that we forget just how many unfriendly skin ingredients they contain.

DEEP-FRIED FOODS

These are a source of heated oils and trans fats that are highly inflammatory and high in the ageing free radicals that cause cellular damage. This is because oils that have been heated at such high temperatures become oxidative and then form free radicals. Ideally we want to try to avoid free radicals as much as possible because they are known to destroy or age cells, blemishes can appear more frequently and fine lines can become more visible.

FIZZY DRINKS

These are packed with refined sugar and provide absolute zero nutrition but plenty of artificial chemicals and preservatives. The diet versions aren't any better as they disrupt healthy gut bacteria.

10 Happy Skin Kitchen Principles

Before we dive into the recipes, I want to share with you my principles or 'guidelines', which I hope will provide a helpful guide as you start this new way of eating, and I am confident they will quickly become second nature. These are not meant to be strict or rigid rules – simply some practical tips to help you make healthier choices that your body and your skin will thank you for.

1. NUTRIENT-DENSE OVER CALORIES: Lay off counting the calories and focus on counting the nutrients instead. Not all calories are created equal. For example, 100 calories of broccoli might deliver the same energy as 100 calories of sweets but they are fundamentally different. Broccoli contains antioxidants, minerals, vitamins and fibre, while sweets have barely any nutrition at all. Which one do you think your skin will benefit from?

2. SHOP SEASONALLY: Buy locally grown and seasonal produce as much as possible, to get maximum nourishment as well as good value. Seasonal foods are usually cheaper, fresher and more nutrient-dense, as they don't have to travel across the world to reach your table and they get picked at peak ripeness.

3. EAT THE RAINBOW: Think scarlet bell peppers, purple cabbage, bright-pink strawberries and forest-green kale. These eye-catching colours are all signs of different phytochemicals, powerful chemical compounds found in plant foods. Phytochemicals are wonderful for our health and our beauty and we should eat as many different kinds (colours) as possible.

4. GET ORGANIZED: Take a little time each week to stock up your fridge and pantry with nourishing ingredients. Also, a little meal prepping or some batch cooking can go a long way, especially if you have a busy schedule. Having a few delicious snacks and meals ready to go in the fridge will make eating a wholesome diet so much easier.

5. COOK 90 PER CENT OF YOUR MEALS FROM SCRATCH: There is no denying that the healthiest meals you eat are always the ones you cook from scratch, because you are fully in control of exactly what goes into them. It's also a great way to get experimenting and create your own beautifying recipes.

6. STAY HYDRATED: Many people underestimate the power of drinking water and the positive effects it can have on your skin. Drinking more water is one the easiest ways to get that glowing skin we all want. I aim to drink 3 litres of water every day, and I often reach for herbal infusions, which make the task so much easier and tastier.

7. ADD SOME GREENS AT LUNCH AND DINNER: Greens are one of the most nutrient-dense foods on the planet and they are one of the most powerful beauty foods. Add a handful of rocket to your lunchbox or stir a handful of spinach through your pasta sauce. It's so much easier than you think, and it will quickly become second nature.

8. EAT SOME FORM OF FERMENTED FOOD EACH DAY: Eating fermented foods is the easiest and cheapest way to boost your meals with some gut-loving probiotics.

9. SLOW DOWN: Take time to enjoy your meals, don't just wolf down your food in front of the computer or while scrolling on social media. Try to make mealtime an occasion when you really connect with what you are eating and the goodness it is providing.

10. FIND JOY: Always enjoy and savour what you choose to eat. Find what works for you and your beauty and don't strive for 'perfection' every time. Remember, what we eat 90 per cent of the time is what matters, and food should always be fun and not something we feel guilty about.

The following pages contain more than 110 plant-based and gluten-free recipes that are delicious, nutritious, and that have been created to support and nourish your skin with every morsel. I hope that no matter what food philosophy you follow, you will love and benefit from these recipes and I hope this book will equip you with the knowledge and confidence to make choices that lead to radiant, happy and youthful skin.

Glow Getter Breakfasts

Without a doubt breakfast is my favourite meal of the day. As soon as I wake up, I start dreaming about what delicious delights I am going to have that day. It's a cliché, but making the decision to eat well in the morning really sets the tone for the whole day. For me, it's vital to get up 10 minutes earlier to whip up a nourishing and nutritious breakfast that will power me through any busy day. A healthy and balanced breakfast doesn't have to take hours to prepare. Most of the recipes in this chapter are pretty quick and others can be made in advance – ideal for those super-rushed mornings.

"Deciding first thing in the morning to look after yourself and your skin is a powerful habit that will make you feel good about yourself from the get-go."

From a skin point of view, starting your day with a good dose of vitamins, fibre, healthy fats and proteins means you will have plenty of energy to get you started and keep you going until lunchtime. The slow release of energy means that you won't get sugar spikes or energy crashes. Higher blood sugar levels have been linked to both acne and ageing skin. One of the best ways to stop sugar spikes is to focus on fibre-rich wholefoods, which naturally act to stabilize blood sugar levels. For example, the high fibre content of many fruits is the reason why the sugar in whole fruits is absorbed at a more stable rate into the bloodstream compared to refined sugar.

Personally, if I don't have a filling breakfast I find myself snacking and picking at food in between meals. When I am really ravenous I will literally eat anything that's in front of me and that's usually when all my healthy eating habits go out of the window. Having a nourishing breakfast has therefore quickly become a non-negotiable ritual for me.

I also think that from an emotional and mental point of view, deciding first thing in the morning to look after yourself and your skin is a powerful habit that will make you feel good about yourself from the get-go. Once you've made that decision at breakfast you are more likely to be inspired to keep going on a positive path with a nutritious lunch and dinner.

Only a few years ago I used to drag myself out of bed, rush to the coffee shop, order a cappuccino and a croissant and would eat nothing else until lunch. My energy would crash after only an hour or so and I would just gargle down more coffee to keep me going. Coffee was probably one of my main food groups around that time, as I consistently relied on it for energy. I clearly wasn't nourishing myself properly because I found myself constantly hungry or peckish. It's only since I changed my diet that I realized the incredible power of a morning routine and starting my day with the best fuel. Long gone are the energy dips and the constant yawns in front of my computer. Since I started eating balanced and nutritious meals, I am a much more active and energetic person, and of course my skin is much happier too!

What I eat for breakfast changes according to the seasons. In winter I find myself craving warming dishes like my Cacao, Buckwheat & Pear Porridge or my Mushroom & Cavolo Nero Toast. During the summer I might crave something a bit lighter, like my Bircher Muesli or my Buckwheat Crispies. My favourite recipes for when I have a little extra time on my hands are my Fluffy Wholegrain Pancakes and my Baked Double Chocolate, Raspberry & Hazelnut Oats. If you have a super-busy schedule and struggle to find the time to have breakfast, my Granola Cookies (page 272) are a weekday wonder.

Bircher Muesli Three Ways

When I first transitioned to a plant-centric diet, the first thing I changed was my breakfast. Instead of getting my daily croissant and Starbucks cappuccino, I started making Bircher muesli so I could grab it from the fridge and eat it on my way to work. Bircher muesli has held a place in my heart ever since, because it is so easy and quick to make and it's a great vessel for packing in lots of goodness and, of course, flavour! Oats are an often overlooked food, but they contain both soluble and insoluble fibre. Soluble fibre forms a viscous gel that helps to lower cholesterol and stabilize blood glucose levels. The insoluble fibre promotes regularity by curtailing constipation and improving intestinal health, which is so important for clear and happy skin. This Bircher trifecta are all delicious as they are, but feel free to serve them with any toppings of your choice.

If you are having these as a breakfast on-the-go, you can split the Bircher into two jars before putting them into the fridge.

They will all store well in the fridge for 3–4 days.

SERVES 2

250ml plant milk of your choice
(I have used almond)
½ tsp vanilla bean paste
2 tbsp almond butter
3 Medjool dates, pitted
100g porridge oats
1 tbsp chia seeds

SERVE WITH:

extra almond butter, coconut yogurt, fruit or any toppings of your choice!

ALMOND BUTTER & DATE

This Bircher muesli is unexpectedly decadent. The creamy almond butter and juicy dates create the most rich and delicious flavour when blended and mixed with the almond milk and oats. It's pretty incredible as it is, but I like to serve it with some seasonal fruit for an extra burst of freshness.

Put the milk, vanilla bean paste, almond butter and two of the dates into a blender. Blend until smooth and creamy. In a large bowl mix together the oats, chia seeds and the remaining date, chopped into pieces. Pour over the blended milk and mix everything together. Place in the fridge overnight or for at least 2–3 hours, until gloopy and creamy.

STRAWBERRY & CREAM

You really can't beat the combination of juicy strawberries and creamy coconut milk. The oats get soaked in this seductive strawberry 'milkshake', which transforms them into the sublime. These will bring joy to any breakfast table.

SERVES 2

250ml coconut milk (from a carton)
½ tsp vanilla bean paste
1 heaped tbsp coconut yogurt
10 strawberries
100g porridge oats
1 tbsp chia seeds

SERVE WITH:

extra coconut yogurt, chopped strawberries,
   or any toppings of your choice!

Put the milk, vanilla bean paste, coconut yogurt and 5 strawberries into a blender, and blend until smooth and creamy.

In a large bowl mix together the oats, chia seeds and the remaining strawberries, chopped into small pieces. Pour in the strawberry milk and combine everything together.

Place in the fridge overnight or for at least 2–3 hours, until gloopy and creamy.

APPLE & GINGER

This is definitely my favourite Bircher muesli to make in autumn, when I find myself craving warming spices. The cinnamon and apple duets delightfully alongside the creamy oats and raisins, to add the perfect amount of sweetness. I often serve it with some creamy almond butter and some extra sliced apple.

SERVES 2

100g porridge oats
1 tbsp chia seeds
1 apple, grated
1 tsp ground cinnamon
½ tsp ground ginger
2 tbsp raisins
1 tbsp sunflower seeds
250ml plant milk of your choice
   (I have used coconut)

SERVE WITH:

a dollop of nut butter
extra sliced apples or any toppings
   of your choice!

Simply put all the ingredients into a large bowl. Mix everything well together and place it in the fridge overnight or for at least 2–3 hours, until gloopy and creamy. Serve with your favourite toppings.

Porridge Two Ways

Porridge is definitely one of my go-to breakfasts, especially during the colder months when a piping hot bowl of creamy comfort food feels like a cosy warm blanket. I also think that porridge can be the perfect vehicle to load up on nutrition in an effortless and affordable way. I switch up my oats by using different grains like quinoa and buckwheat, which both provide wonderful skin minerals and antioxidants and taste delicious too.

SERVES 2

150g buckwheat grains, soaked
  overnight in cold water
250ml coconut milk (from
  a carton)
4 dates, pitted and chopped into
  small pieces
1 tsp vanilla bean paste
2 tbsp raw cacao powder
1 tbsp coconut sugar
1 pear, core removed and cut
  into slices
½ tsp ground cinnamon

SERVE WITH:

a sprinkle of chopped pistachios
a sprinkle of hemp seeds

CACAO, BUCKWHEAT & PEAR PORRIDGE

Despite having 'wheat' in its name, buckwheat is actually a seed and is sometimes referred to as a 'pseudo-grain'. Buckwheat has an enviable antioxidant profile, better than that of many common cereal grains like oats or wheat. As well as containing plant compounds like rutin, which decreases the formation of wrinkle-promoting AGEs in the body, it is also a great source of quercetin, another powerful antioxidant. I love pairing it with the richness of the raw cacao, the sweetness of the dates and the caramel-like flavour of the stewed pears. It's truly a nourishing bowl for cold and dark mornings.

Drain the buckwheat grains and rinse them well until all the slimy water has disappeared. Put the buckwheat, coconut milk, chopped dates, vanilla bean paste and raw cacao powder into a pan on a medium heat. Cook for 20–25 minutes, until all the liquid has been absorbed and your porridge is creamy and gloopy. Make sure to keep stirring from time to time, to prevent it sticking to the bottom of the pan. I like mine quite thick, but if you prefer a runnier consistency, feel free to add a bit more milk or water.

While the porridge cooks, prepare the pear. Put the coconut sugar and 3 tablespoons of water into a pan on a medium heat. Mix the coconut sugar with the water and when it starts to bubble, add the sliced pear. Toss the pear around so it gets evenly coated in the syrup. Sprinkle the ground cinnamon on top and cook the pear for a few minutes until it starts to soften but still has a little bounce.

Serve the porridge with the cooked pear and a sprinkle of chopped pistachios and hemp seeds.

60g quinoa
300ml coconut milk (from
   a carton)
1 tsp vanilla bean paste
60g porridge oats
2 tbsp maple syrup (optional)

FOR THE RASPBERRY CHIA JAM:

170g frozen or fresh raspberries
1 tbsp chia seeds

SERVE WITH:

a spoonful of peanut butter
a handful of fresh raspberries

OAT AND QUINOA PEANUT BUTTER & JELLY PORRIDGE

I have tried to make porridge with only quinoa in the past and I felt it was never really creamy enough. This porridge is the best of both worlds. The combination of peanut butter, chia seeds and quinoa results in a healthy dose of plant protein, and all the creaminess you crave from the oat flakes. You can top it with whatever you prefer, but my Raspberry Chia Jam and a generous drizzle of peanut butter are my top picks.

Make the raspberry chia jam by putting the raspberries into a pan on a medium heat with a dash of water to prevent them from burning. Cook the raspberries for around 10 minutes, until they have gone mushy and you have a jam kind of consistency. Turn off the heat and add the chia seeds. Stir everything together and leave it to one side to cool down and thicken up.

Rinse the quinoa and put it into a pan on a medium heat together with the coconut milk and vanilla bean paste. Once it starts to boil, turn the heat down and cover it with a lid. Cook the quinoa for 10–15 minutes, until most of the milk has been absorbed and the quinoa seeds are starting to bloom. Add the porridge oats, maple syrup (if using) and 200ml of water (if you want it extra creamy you can also use more coconut milk). Stir everything together and cook for 5–8 more minutes, until the porridge is creamy and gloopy. Add a bit more liquid if needed.

Serve the porridge with a generous dollop of the raspberry chia jam, some peanut butter and a scattering of fresh raspberries.

Chickpea Pancake with Black Beans & Mushrooms

I have been making variations of this chickpea pancake for years and it is still a favourite of mine. It not only tastes absolutely delicious but it is also a super easy way to pack in a wide variety of plants in one meal. Plant diversity is key to optimal gut health, so the higher the number of different plant-based foods you eat, the more diverse your gut bacteria. And this diversity is linked not just to better gut health but to overall health too, including heart, brain and, you guessed it – skin health! This recipe packs in a minimum of six different types of plants, lots of fibre, protein, and of course lots of flavour too! It's the prefect fuss-free recipe, which is great for breakfast, lunch or dinner. I love serving it with creamy avocado, fresh spring onions and a sprinkle of coriander.

MAKES 1 LARGE PANCAKE (ENOUGH FOR 1)

FOR THE PANCAKE:

30g chickpea flour (also called gram flour)
½ tbsp nutritional yeast
¼ tsp ground turmeric
¼ tsp smoked paprika
a pinch each of salt and pepper

FOR THE FILLING:

olive oil, for cooking
½ a red onion, finely chopped
100g cherry tomatoes, cut in half
70g cooked black beans
50g chestnut mushrooms, sliced
1 tsp smoked paprika
1 tbsp tamari sauce
a handful of baby spinach
½ a ripe avocado
1 spring onion, finely chopped
a squeeze of lime juice
a sprinkle of chopped fresh coriander
salt and pepper, to taste

Start by making the batter for the pancake. Put the chickpea flour into a large bowl with the nutritional yeast, turmeric, smoked paprika and salt and pepper. Mix everything together. Pour in 70ml of cold water and combine all the ingredients, using a whisk. Make sure to whisk vigorously in order to have a smooth batter and to break down any lumps. Leave it to one side.

Put a drizzle of olive oil into a frying pan on a medium heat and, once hot, add the chopped onion. Cook for 5–8 minutes, until it starts to caramelize. Add the cherry tomatoes, stir everything together, and cook for another 5 minutes, until the tomatoes start to burst. Add the black beans, mushrooms, smoked paprika and tamari sauce and cook for 8–10 more minutes, until the mushrooms are cooked. Finally add the baby spinach and cook for 1–2 minutes, until wilted.

In the meantime, cook the pancake. Put a drizzle of olive oil into a non-stick pan on a medium heat. Once the pan is very hot, pour in the pancake batter, tipping the mixture around the pan to form a very thin layer. This kind of pancake can be really fragile, so make sure you cook it on one side for at least 5 minutes before flipping it on to the other side to finish for another 5 minutes.

While the pancake is cooking, mash the avocado in a bowl and add the spring onion, lime juice and a pinch of salt. Mix until you have a creamy guacamole.

Transfer the pancake to a plate, spread the guacamole on top, add some chopped coriander, then the black beans and mushrooms, and fold it over before serving.

Granola Two Ways

I am a big fan of granola for breakfast – it is such a speedy and divine option. Sadly, most store-bought granolas are loaded with sugar, making them a skin enemy, especially first thing in the morning. These granolas are subtly sweet. I really wanted them to be super-nutritious and packed with lots of beauty vitamins and minerals without being too sugary, but of course still delicious!

MAKES A 500ML JAR

220g buckwheat grains, soaked
   for a couple of hours (this will
   help soften the grains)
20g pumpkin seeds
20g sunflower seeds
30g flaked almonds
30g coconut chips
30g coconut oil, melted
3 tbsp maple syrup
1 tsp vanilla bean paste
a pinch of sea salt

VANILLA BUCKWHEAT CRISPIES

These buckwheat crispies are immense – they remind me of my childhood cereal, just with a significant nutrition overhaul! Buckwheat (which has nothing to do with wheat by the way!) has a nutty flavour and it certainly packs a punch when it comes to skin nutrition. Buckwheat's main phytochemical, rutin, has powerful antioxidant properties and it also helps your body produce collagen. I love pairing buckwheat with mineral-dense seeds like pumpkin seeds. They are rich in zinc, which can help to prevent breakouts. Naturally sweet coconut chips make this granola a ray of sunshine on your plate.

To complement the tropical notes of the coconut, try this granola with coconut yogurt and tangy and fresh passion fruit, though any fruit of your choice will work too.

Preheat the oven to 170°C/150°C fan/gas 3 and line a baking tray with parchment paper.

Drain and rinse the buckwheat grains to get rid of the slimy water. Transfer them to a clean tea towel and pat them dry. Put them into a large bowl with the pumpkin seeds, sunflower seeds, flaked almonds and coconut chips. Mix everything together.

Pour over the melted coconut oil, maple syrup, vanilla bean paste and add a pinch of salt. Combine well.

Spread the buckwheat granola on the lined baking tray and bake in the oven for 45 minutes. When they are 20 minutes in, remove the tray and give the granola a stir. Put it back in the oven for the final 25 minutes.

Remove from the oven and let the granola cool down completely (very important, otherwise it will get soggy), then transfer it to a jar. Stores well for 3–4 weeks.

8 Medjool dates, pitted
60g runny and smooth almond
  butter
200g rolled oats
60g mixed nuts (I have used a
  mix of walnuts and pecans)
20g sunflower seeds
20g pumpkin seeds
1 tbsp ground cinnamon
a pinch of sea salt
15g solid coconut oil, melted

NUTTY DATE GRANOLA

Crunchy and nutty, this granola is brilliant for breakfast but also works well as a snack, as you get some generous-size clusters. To sweeten this granola, I only used Medjool dates, which in my opinion are nature's caramel candies. Despite their sugar content, dates contain some important vitamins and minerals, in addition to significant amounts of fibre. Pair them with the buttery and rich flavour of the almond butter and it creates the most indulgent combination, yet so full of goodness! Almonds are rich in vitamin E, which keeps skin moisturized and protected from the sun's harmful rays. Serve this granola with almond milk and chopped apples, as they really complement the warm flavour of the cinnamon.

Preheat the oven to 170°C/150°C fan/gas 3 and line a large baking tray with parchment paper.

Put the Medjool dates, 70ml of cold water and the almond butter into a blender and blend until you have a creamy and fairly smooth paste. In a large bowl, mix the oats, mixed nuts, sunflower seeds, pumpkin seeds, cinnamon and salt. Add the date and almond paste and mix everything together. Finally, add the melted coconut oil and stir to combine. Spread the granola on the lined baking tray and bake in the oven for 20 minutes.

Remove the tray and give the granola a stir. Bake for a further 20 minutes, then remove from the oven. Let the granola cool down completely (very important, otherwise it will get soggy) before transferring into a jar. Stores well for 3–4 weeks.

Baked Double Chocolate, Raspberry & Hazelnut Oats

This is the perfect breakfast for those days when getting out of bed is a real struggle. Baked oats are a true revelation – you would never imagine they could taste so good! Oats are a power-house of nutrients, and thanks to their high fibre content they will support gut health and will keep you feeling fuller for longer. Oats are also a good source of selenium, which supports skin elasticity and firmness, as well as helping to protect it from sun damage. Raw cacao not only makes these oats taste like you are having pudding for breakfast but it also provides a hefty dose of antioxidants, which are essential in fighting free radicals and premature ageing. The tart, fresh raspberries go so well with the richness of the cacao and also add extra vitamin C to the dish. Hazelnuts and chocolate are best friends, but if you can't get your hands on them, almonds and walnuts work really well too.

SERVES 2

1 very ripe banana
120g porridge oats
2 tbsp maple syrup
300ml plant milk of your choice
    (I have used almond)
1 tsp vanilla bean paste
2 tbsp nut butter of your choice
    (I have used almond)
2 tbsp raw cacao powder
30g good quality dark chocolate
    (I love to use 70–80% cocoa),
    cut into small pieces
100g raspberries
20g hazelnuts, roughly chopped
a drizzle of nut butter of your
    choice (optional), to serve

Preheat the oven to 200°C/180°C fan/gas 6.

Put the banana, oats, maple syrup, plant milk, vanilla bean paste, nut butter and raw cacao powder into a blender. Blend until smooth, then transfer to an ovenproof dish. Scatter the chocolate pieces on top and add the raspberries, using them to push the chocolate down into the oats. This way, you will have gooey pockets of chocolate within the oats. Sprinkle with the chopped hazelnuts and bake in the oven for 20 minutes.

Remove from the oven and serve while still hot, with a drizzle of nut butter (if using).

Savoury Breakfast Toasts Three Ways

I know it can be hard to think of a speedy savoury breakfast that isn't mashed avocado on toast, so I wanted to share three of my staples. These are all wonderfully simple and come together in less than 15 minutes, plus they make brilliant lunches too if you are pressed for time. They all pack a good amount of vegetables and fibre in, perfect to feed your skin with vitamins and minerals from the get-go. For these recipes I love using my Nutrient-dense Bread (page 226), but any bread of your choice will work too.

SERVES 2

2 tbsp extra virgin olive oil + extra
   for drizzling
150g mixed mushrooms, sliced
   (I love to use shiitake and
   chestnut mushrooms)
2 garlic cloves, crushed
1 tbsp balsamic vinegar
a few sprigs of thyme
40g cavolo nero, stem removed
   and leaves chopped
2 tbsp unsweetened coconut
   yogurt
2 tbsp plant milk of your choice
   (I have used oat)
salt and pepper, to taste
2 slices of toast, to serve

MUSHROOM & CAVOLO NERO

I make this recipe all the time because it's easy-peasy but so full of flavour. I just adore the contrast between the silkiness of the coconut yogurt and the earthiness of the mushrooms. I generally add some vibrant greens for extra antioxidants and vitamin A.

Put the olive oil into a large pan on a medium heat. Once hot, add the sliced mushrooms and sauté for 5 minutes. Add the crushed garlic and cook for another minute. Add the balsamic vinegar and thyme leaves and stir everything together. Add the cavolo nero and cook for another 2–3 minutes, until it starts to wilt. Add the coconut yogurt and plant milk, and season with salt and pepper. Cook for a final 2 minutes. Divide between the 2 slices of toast and serve.

1 tbsp olive oil
½ a red onion, chopped really
    finely
200g cherry tomatoes, cut in
    halves
½ x 400g tin of chickpeas,
    drained and rinsed
1 tbsp harissa paste
salt and pepper, to taste
extra virgin olive oil, for drizzling
2 slices of toast, to serve

HARISSA, TOMATO & CHICKPEAS

This is the most filling option out of the three, fab for those mornings
when you need extra fuel to power you through a busy day. The
chickpeas add a hefty dose of plant protein and fibre, great to stabilize
your blood sugar levels. The fiery harissa really brings everything to
life and it's perfectly balanced by the sweetness of the tomatoes. This
also makes great leftovers, so feel free to double the quantities.

Put the olive oil into a frying pan on a medium heat. Once hot, add
the chopped onion and cook for 5–8 minutes, until the onion starts
to caramelize. Add the tomatoes and cook for 5 minutes, until the
tomatoes have softened. Add the chickpeas and harissa paste, stir
everything together and cook for the final 5 minutes. Season with
salt and pepper, divide between the 2 slices of toast and serve with
a little drizzle of extra virgin olive oil.

70g frozen edamame beans
1 ripe avocado, peeled, stoned
    and roughly chopped
juice of ½ a lime
1 garlic clove, crushed
a small handful of fresh
    coriander, finely chopped
a pinch of salt
100g tomatoes, chopped into
    small pieces
a handful of my Sauerkraut
    (page 256)
a drizzle of extra virgin olive oil
2 slices of toast, to serve

SUPERCHARGED AVOCADO

As the name suggests, this is my supercharged version of the classic
avocado on toast. The addition of edamame beans makes this toast
immediately more satiating and filling. To add a zing of freshness,
I pair it with some fresh tomatoes and a forkful of my sauerkraut,
which will also give you your daily dose of gut-loving probiotics.

Put the edamame beans into a heatproof bowl and cover them with
plenty of boiling water. Let them sit for 5 minutes, until they are soft.
Put them into a blender or food processor with the avocado, lime
juice, garlic, coriander and a pinch of salt. Blend everything together
until smooth and creamy. Divide the spread between the 2 slices of
toast and top with the chopped tomatoes, sauerkraut and a drizzle of
extra virgin olive oil.

Fluffy Wholegrain Pancakes

Pancakes are usually a weekend treat, but these wholesome pancakes are jam-packed with that much goodness, you would be forgiven for wanting them every day. Thanks to the oat and buckwheat flour they are high in fibre, which will help balance blood sugar levels and keep you feeling full until lunchtime.

Buckwheat is a brilliant gluten-free flour – it has a delicious nutty flavour, it's rich in important minerals like iron and magnesium, plus it's a great source of protein. I kept these pancakes lightly sweet, as I didn't want them to become a sugar-laden breakfast. I enjoy them with my Spiced Berry Compote (page 214), but they are also incredibly delicious with a drizzle of nut butter and some fresh berries.

MAKES 6 PANCAKES

75g oat flour
50g buckwheat flour
1 tsp bicarbonate of soda
½ tsp baking powder
a pinch of salt
150ml plant milk of your choice
1 tsp vanilla bean paste
½ tbsp apple cider vinegar
1 tbsp maple syrup
a little bit of coconut oil, for
    cooking

SERVE WITH:

a dollop of my Spiced Berry
    Compote (page 214), or a
    drizzle of nut butter and
    berries of your choice

Put the oat flour, buckwheat flour, bicarbonate of soda, baking powder and salt into a bowl and mix well. In a separate bowl, mix together the plant milk, vanilla bean paste, apple cider vinegar and maple syrup. Pour the wet ingredients into the dry, and mix until well combined. Let the batter sit for 5 minutes to thicken up. This will also ensure fluffier pancakes.

Put the coconut oil into a large frying pan on a medium heat. Once the pan is hot, spoon in about 2 tablespoons of the pancake batter, using the back of the spoon to shape the mix into a circle. Cook on one side for 4–5 minutes, then flip and cook the other side for 2–3 minutes, until cooked through. Keep the cooked pancakes warm on a plate in a very low oven and repeat until all the batter is finished. Serve the pancakes warm, with the spiced berry compote or toppings of your choice.

TIP
These pancakes
are great for freezing.
Simply put them into a
toaster straight from the
freezer for a delicious
breakfast on-the-go or
an afternoon treat.

Happy
Skin Bowls

I am a big fan of nourishing bowls, buddha bowls or, as I like to call them, Happy Skin bowls. To me they are the easiest way to load up on goodness and nourish my skin with a wholesome meal any time of the day. My Happy Skin bowls are delicious one-bowl meals, packed with an array of vitamins, antioxidants and nutrient-dense ingredients, designed to feed your skin and make you feel good. Each of the bowls is a well-balanced mix of complex carbohydrates, plant-based protein, fibre and healthy fats, which will give you energy and make you feel supremely satisfied.

"My Happy Skin Bowls are delicious one-bowl meals designed to feed your skin and make you feel good."

___

In this chapter you will find a versatile mix of easy Happy Skin bowl recipes, perfect for lunch and dinner or even breakfast if that takes your fancy! Each of these recipes has a mix of different vegetables, grains, nuts and seeds, plus a delicious dressing to enhance and bring the ingredients together.

I love building a Happy Skin bowl, as I really get to be creative and play around with different flavours and textures. There are obviously no set rules, so I would encourage you to get experimenting in the kitchen. Personally, I like to keep in mind the following building blocks to ensure my bowl is nutritiously balanced and, of course, incredibly delicious.

WHOLE GRAINS
Quinoa, millet, buckwheat and wild/brown rice are my favourite gluten-free grains, which also bring a good dose of protein. Because they are whole, they are also high in fibre, which means they will give you sustained and slow-released energy throughout the day. Be ready to wave goodbye to that 4 p.m. slump!

PROTEIN
A wholesome source of protein is what gives my bowls extra substance and contributes to that feeling of satiety. My favourite plant-based sources of protein are beans, chickpeas, lentils, tempeh and tofu, which are also all rich in fibre for that fuller-for-longer feeling.

HEALTHY FATS

Healthy fats are essential for supporting healthy, plump and glowing skin, and they also add to that feeling of fullness. I love using creamy avocado or crunchy nuts and seeds to add texture, colour and flavour.

VEGETABLES

Vegetables are the heart and soul of all my Happy Skin bowls and usually make up at least half of the bowl. I love to use a mix of cooked and raw veggies to create delicious textures. A variety of vegetables not only makes a colourful meal but is also a great way to pack in a wide assortment of minerals, vitamins and antioxidants, which your skin will thank you for.

EXTRA SPRINKLES OR GARNISHES

At the end of the chapter you will find three delicious Sprinkle recipes, which are an easy way to boost the nutrition of your bowl as well as inject different flavours and textures. They can all be made in advance and stored in the fridge, so they are good-to-go whenever you feel you want to spruce up a dish. Feel free to finish off your Happy Skin bowl with some gut-loving kimchi or sauerkraut (see pages 252–261), or a sprinkle of fresh herbs for an extra pop of freshness.

DRESSING OR SAUCE

No Happy Skin bowl is complete without a saucy dressing to drizzle on top. This final element is what really brings the bowl to life and ties all the ingredients together. I love making my dressings and sauces from scratch, not only because I think they taste much better than shop-bought ones, but because I can ensure they are all made with wholesome ingredients and contain no refined sugar.

Gado Gado-style Bowl

Tempeh is a fermented soy product that has a lovely nutty flavour and can be used in many dishes, such as stir-fries, curries or salads. It is not only rich in bone-strengthening calcium and anti-inflammatory isoflavones, but it also happens to be gut friendly thanks to the fermentation process, which adds probiotics. For this bowl, I have used a spicy and smoky marinade with a creamy peanut dressing, which ensures the dish is bursting with flavour. I love the variety of crunchy vegetables, perfect for an antioxidant, vitamin and mineral power-up. The buckwheat noodles really add something special, but brown or black rice will work great too.

SERVES 2

FOR THE TEMPEH:
4 tbsp tamari sauce
1 tbsp toasted sesame seed oil
1 tsp rice vinegar
1 tsp maple syrup
½ tbsp chilli sauce
300g tempeh
olive oil, for frying

FOR THE PEANUT DRESSING:
3 tbsp peanut butter
1 tbsp tamari or soy sauce
1 tsp tamarind paste
1 tbsp lime juice
1 tsp maple syrup

FOR THE REST OF THE BOWL:
100g buckwheat or rice noodles
1 carrot, peeled and thinly sliced
½ a cucumber, cut into half-moons
½ a red pepper, cut into thin strips
4–5 radishes, thinly sliced
200g mixed tenderstem and green
    beans, lightly steamed
2 handfuls of lettuce or mixed
    salad greens
2 spring onions, finely chopped

SERVE WITH:
a small handful of salted peanuts,
    roughly chopped
1 red chilli (optional), deseeded
    and cut into thin slices
a small handful of fresh coriander,
    chopped

Make the tempeh marinade. Put the tamari, sesame seed oil, rice vinegar, maple syrup and chilli sauce into a large bowl and mix everything together. Cut the tempeh into slices (about 5mm thick) and add them to the bowl of marinade. Gently toss them around so they get coated. Let the tempeh marinate in the fridge for at least 1 hour, or even better overnight.

Make the dressing. Put all the ingredients into a bowl with 2–3 tablespoons of cold water and mix until you have a runny consistency. Add more water if needed.

Cook the rice noodles according to the packet instructions. Drain and rinse with cold water. Set to one side.

Put a drizzle of olive oil into a frying pan or griddle pan. Once very hot, add the tempeh slices and cook them on each side for 2–3 minutes. Brush the leftover marinade over the cooked tempeh.

To assemble your bowl, put all the chopped veggies into a large bowl, followed by the buckwheat/rice noodles and steamed greens. Add the tempeh slices and drizzle with the peanut sauce. Serve with a sprinkle of salted peanuts, chilli (if using) and some chopped coriander.

Almond Butter & Miso Shiitake Mushroom Bowl

Shiitake mushrooms are known for their immune-supporting properties and they also provide bags of iron, B vitamins and selenium, a trace mineral that protects our skin's elasticity. I absolutely adore the 'meaty' texture and earthy taste profile of shiitake mushrooms, and I think they particularly shine when paired with strong-flavoured ingredients like brown rice miso paste, tamari sauce and rich almond butter. I often serve them with fluffy quinoa and jewel-green cavolo nero, which will also provide you with a good dose of skin-loving vitamin A and antioxidants. To add texture I love a generous sprinkle of my Almond & Hazelnut Dukkah (page 104), which is also a wonderful way to boost your intake of vitamin E.

SERVES 2

100g quinoa
2 tbsp brown miso paste
2 tbsp toasted sesame seed oil +
    extra for roasting
½ tbsp tamari sauce
1 tsp mirin
2 tsp rice vinegar
240g shiitake mushrooms, sliced
    (if you have any tiny ones you
    can leave them whole)
2 tbsp almond butter
50g cavolo nero or curly kale,
    de-stemmed and finely sliced
a drizzle of olive oil, for cooking
1 garlic clove, crushed
salt and pepper, to taste

SERVE WITH:

a couple of spring onions, finely
    chopped
a couple of radishes, thinly sliced
a squeeze of lime juice
a sprinkle of my Almond &
    Hazelnut Dukkah (page 104)

TIP
If you are not a
big fan of radishes,
try thinly sliced
carrots instead.

Preheat the oven to 220°C/200°C fan/gas 7 and line a large baking tray with parchment paper.

Cook the quinoa according to the packet instructions. Set aside.

In a bowl, whisk together the miso paste, toasted sesame seed oil, tamari sauce, mirin and rice vinegar, to make a marinade.

Put the sliced mushrooms into a large bowl, then pour over the majority of the marinade, making sure you reserve about ½ tablespoon for the dressing. Mix the mushrooms well, until they are evenly coated in the marinade.

Spread the mushrooms on the lined baking tray, making sure there is space between them, so they will become nice and crispy. Drizzle with some extra toasted sesame oil, then roast in the oven for 20 minutes, until golden.

While the mushrooms are cooking, add the almond butter to the reserved marinade together with 3 tablespoons of cold water. Mix everything together until smooth, adding a bit more water for a runnier consistency if necessary. Set the dressing on one side.

To cook the cavolo nero, put a drizzle of olive oil (about 1 tablespoon) into a large frying pan. Once hot, add the cavolo nero and cook on a medium heat for 3–5 minutes. Add a dash of water, stir and add the crushed garlic. Cook for another 1–2 minutes, making sure you keep stirring to prevent the garlic from burning.

To assemble your bowl, add the quinoa as the base, followed by the cavolo nero and the miso mushrooms. Add some chopped spring onions and sliced radishes, drizzle with the almond butter dressing, and add a squeeze of lime juice and a sprinkle of the dukkah.

Mexican Tofu Scramble & Quinoa Power Bowl

I like to call this my Power Bowl because it is truly a powerhouse of nutrients and it always manages to fuel me through the most manic of days. Quinoa is a complete plant-based source of protein, high in fibre, iron and magnesium, as well as rich in those mighty antioxidants. Don't be put off by the seemingly long list of ingredients (I am sure most of them are already in your cupboard) – all the different elements are what makes this bowl so utterly delicious and jam-packed with flavour and texture.

SERVES 2

50g quinoa
160g firm tofu
1 tbsp nutritional yeast
1 tsp garlic powder
½ tsp ground turmeric
a dash of plant milk of your choice
1 spring onion, finely chopped

FOR THE SALSA:
½ a red onion, finely sliced
200g cherry tomatoes, chopped
½ tbsp olive oil
juice of ½ a lime
a small handful of fresh coriander, finely chopped
salt and pepper, to taste

FOR THE BEANS:
1 tbsp olive oil
1 shallot, finely chopped
2 garlic cloves, crushed
1 chilli, finely chopped
1 tsp smoked paprika
1 tsp dried or fresh oregano
250g cooked mixed beans, drained and rinsed
2 tbsp tomato purée
1 tsp apple cider vinegar
1 tsp coconut sugar
salt and pepper, to taste

SERVE WITH:
a handful of mixed greens
1 avocado, mashed and seasoned with a pinch of salt and pepper
a sprinkle of chopped fresh coriander

Make the salsa by mixing all the ingredients in a bowl. Season with salt and pepper and set aside.

Cook the quinoa according to the packet instructions. Set aside.

While the quinoa is cooking, get on with the beans. Put the olive oil into a large frying pan on a medium heat. Once hot, add the chopped shallot and cook for 5–8 minutes, until transparent and slightly caramelized. Add the crushed garlic, chilli, smoked paprika and oregano and cook for another 2 minutes, stirring continuously to prevent the garlic from burning. Add the beans, tomato purée, apple cider vinegar, coconut sugar and 150ml of water. Stir everything together, turn down to a simmer, cover with a lid and cook for 20–25 minutes, until the sauce has slightly thickened.

In the meantime, crumble the tofu with your hands and put it into a separate pan. Add the nutritional yeast, garlic powder, turmeric and plant milk so it doesn't stick to the pan. Cook the tofu on a medium heat for 5 minutes. Then add the cooked quinoa, chopped spring onion, season with salt and pepper and stir to combine.

To assemble, place a layer of the mixed greens in the bottom of each bowl, followed by the tofu and quinoa scramble, spicy beans, salsa and mashed avocado. Serve with a sprinkle of chopped coriander on top.

Notes: You can use pre-cooked quinoa to speed up the cooking time. The beans are suitable for freezing and are a great addition to bulk up any meal. They are also delicious on toast!

Spicy Roots & Millet Bowl With a Herby Yogurt Dressing

Millet is one of those completely underrated pseudo-grains (technically it is a seed). It's naturally gluten-free, extremely affordable and packs some serious nutritional oomph. Millet is particularly rich in antioxidants, especially ferulic acid and catechins. These molecules act to protect your body and your skin from oxidative stress, which can contribute to ageing. I love pairing this fluffy grain with spicy and smoky starchy vegetables, which make this bowl so filling and satisfying. Carrot and butternut squash are a great source of beta-carotene, which gets converted in the body into vitamin A, a powerful vitamin which helps to smooth skin texture and protect it against harmful UV rays.

The fiery harissa is beautifully balanced by the cooling coconut yogurt dressing that is also sensational with salads or as a dip. Serve with a sprinkle of my Almond & Hazelnut Dukkah (see page 104) for an extra crunchy bite and some skin-loving fats.

SERVES 2

100g millet, drained and rinsed
1 red onion, cut into quarters
2 carrots, cut into chunks
200g butternut squash or
    pumpkin, cut into cubes
    (skin on)
1 beetroot, cut into chunks
2 tbsp harissa paste
a drizzle of olive oil
1 red pepper, deseeded and
    chopped
½ x 400g tin of chickpeas, drained
    and rinsed
salt and pepper, to taste

FOR THE DRESSING:

100g plain coconut yogurt
juice of ½ a lemon
1 tbsp extra virgin olive oil
1 garlic clove, crushed
a handful (about 10g) of chopped
    fresh mint
a handful (about 10g) of chopped
    fresh coriander
salt and pepper, to taste

SERVE WITH:

a generous sprinkle of my Almond
    & Hazelnut Dukkah (page 104)
    or some toasted pumpkin seeds
a sprinkle of chopped fresh
    coriander

Preheat the oven to 220°C/200°C fan/gas 7.

Cook the millet according to the packet instructions. My favourite way to cook millet is to put it into a large pan, cover it with plenty of boiling water with a pinch of salt (similar to pasta), and cook it for around 20 minutes, until the seeds are soft. I drain it, let it cool slightly, then fluff it up with a fork.

Put all the chopped vegetables apart from the pepper on a large baking tray. Toss the vegetables with the harissa paste so they get evenly coated. Drizzle with some olive oil and roast in the oven for 25 minutes. Remove the tray, add the chopped red pepper and scatter over the chickpeas. Mix everything together and place it back in the oven for another 15 minutes, until all the vegetables are soft and slightly crispy around the edges.

To make the dressing, just put everything into a small bowl and mix well until smooth.

To assemble, use the cooked millet as the base of your bowl, top it with the roasted vegetables and chickpeas, then drizzle with the yogurt dressing, sprinkle over some dukkah and finally add some chopped coriander.

TIP
This bowl is wonderful hot, warm and even cold in your lunchbox the next day. You can also prep the three elements (millet, roasted vegetables and dressing) ahead of time and just throw it together for the perfect speedy lunch or supper.

Quinoa & Kale Falafels

Thanks to the mushrooms, these falafels are 'meaty' and full of unctuous umami flavours. They are also a plant-based powerhouse, thanks to the mighty quinoa, which is rich in vitamins, antioxidants and minerals such as calcium and iron, essential for strong nails and healthy hair. I add kale for some beautifying vitamin A, which helps to speed up cell turnover for younger-looking skin. These veggie balls are a great addition to any salad, but I particularly love them with the creamy pea purée, which gives an incredible boost of vitamin C to support collagen production and defend your skin from free radicals. I like to serve the falafels with some roasted broccoli, but any roasted vegetables of your choice work too.

MAKES 13–15 FALAFELS, DEPENDING ON THE SIZE

olive oil, for cooking
2 shallots, finely chopped
150g chestnut mushrooms, finely chopped
2 garlic cloves, crushed
1 tbsp tamari sauce
½ tbsp white miso paste
40g kale, de-stemmed and finely chopped
170g cooked quinoa
100g cooked cannellini beans (tinned is fine)
40g ground walnuts
a handful (about 10g) of fresh parsley (stalks removed), finely chopped
1 tbsp nutritional yeast
2 tbsp oat flour

FOR THE PEA PURÉE:

300g frozen peas
2 tbsp extra virgin olive oil
juice of 1 lemon
a small handful of fresh mint leaves (about 5g)
salt and pepper, to taste

SERVE WITH:

200g tenderstem broccoli
a sprinkle of chilli flakes (optional)

Drizzle a little olive oil into a frying pan on a medium heat. Once hot, add the shallots and cook for 5 minutes, until they start to caramelize. Add the chopped mushrooms and crushed garlic, stir everything together, and cook for another 10 minutes until all the water from the mushrooms has evaporated.

Add the tamari sauce, miso paste and chopped kale, stir everything together, and cook for another 2–3 minutes until the kale has wilted. Transfer everything to a food processor together with the cooked quinoa and cannellini beans, ground walnuts, parsley and nutritional yeast. Pulse for few seconds, until you have a dough kind of mixture. Make sure not to over-process, as you don't want a purée consistency.

Transfer the falafel mix into a bowl and add the oat flour. Mix everything together and with wet hands roll the mixture into golf-ball-size balls. Put them on the lined baking tray and place them in the fridge for 20 minutes to firm up.

Preheat the oven to 200°C/180°C fan/gas 6 and line a large baking tray with parchment paper.

Remove the falafel balls from the fridge and bake in the oven for 20 minutes. To the same tray (if you haven't got space, use another tray) add the tenderstem broccoli. Drizzle it with some olive oil, a pinch each of salt and pepper and roast it together with the falafels.

In the meantime, make the pea purée. Blanch the peas in boiling water for 5 minutes, until soft. Drain, then put them into a blender with the extra virgin olive oil, lemon juice, mint, season with salt and pepper and blend until smooth and creamy.

Spread a generous layer of pea purée in each bowl, followed by the falafels and the roasted broccoli, and chilli flakes (if using).

Hummus Bowl with Harissa Peppers & Olive Gremolata

I have hummus pretty much daily. It's a super-versatile dip, and it's a great way to up your plant-based protein and fibre intake. Thanks to one of its key ingredients – tahini – you also get plenty of minerals like zinc and calcium, which are important for strong and healthy nails. This bowl takes the humble hummus to the next level, making it into something extra delectable. Pairing it with the sweet and spicy harissa peppers, salty olives and capers, fresh parsley and some buttery walnuts for a delicious crunch is true bliss. The red peppers are a great source of vitamin C, which is essential in helping boost collagen production for plump and firm skin. This bowl is also not in short supply of healthy fats, thanks to tahini and walnuts, particularly omega-3 fatty acids, which help to strengthen the skin barrier.

SERVES 2

3 red Romano peppers
a drizzle of olive oil, for roasting
70g dried French lentils, rinsed
70g pitted olives (I use a mix of black and green), finely chopped
a handful of parsley (about 10g), chopped very finely
1 tbsp small capers
1 tbsp extra virgin olive oil
1 tbsp lemon juice
1 tbsp harissa paste
30g walnuts, roughly chopped
salt and pepper, to taste

FOR THE HUMMUS:
1 x 400g tin of chickpeas, drained and rinsed
2 tbsp runny tahini
juice of 1 lemon
1 garlic clove
½ tsp ground cumin
3 tbsp extra virgin olive oil
salt, to taste

Preheat the oven to 220°C/200°C fan/gas 7.

Put the whole Romano peppers on a large baking tray. Drizzle with olive oil, sprinkle with salt and pepper, and roast in the oven for 30 minutes, until the peppers are soft and slightly charred on top. Remove from the oven and leave to cool.

In the meantime, put the lentils into a large pan and cover with plenty of boiling water. Cook for 18–20 minutes, until the lentils are soft but not mushy. Drain and set aside.

To make the hummus, simply place all the ingredients in a food processor and blitz until you have a fairly creamy consistency. Then, while the food processor is running, gradually add 4 tablespoons of cold water and keep on blitzing until you have a smooth consistency.

Put the cooked lentils, chopped olives, parsley, capers, extra virgin olive oil and lemon juice into a bowl and mix everything together. Set to one side.

Once the peppers have cooled down, peel off the skin using your hands (it should come off really easily), then remove the seeds and stalks and discard. Mix the pepper flesh in a bowl with the harissa paste and a pinch of salt.

Toast the walnuts in a dry pan on a medium heat for 5–7 minutes, until fragrant.

To assemble, start by spreading a generous layer of hummus at the bottom of each bowl. Add the harissa peppers on top, followed by the olive and lentil gremolata. Finally, sprinkle with the toasted walnuts. Enjoy the bowl as it is or feel free to serve it with some crusty bread.

Summer in a Bowl with a Basil & Walnut Cream

This is the kind of salad that I always make when my dad's garden is overflowing with ripe and sun-drenched tomatoes. The process of slow-roasting tomatoes lifts them to magnificence. Tomatoes are rich in lycopene, which is a powerful antioxidant that can help to protect the skin from UV damage that causes wrinkles, sun spots and fine lines. Cooking tomatoes actually increases the lycopene absorption, as does the addition of a little extra virgin olive oil (rich in vitamin E), so there's even more reason to try this unbeatable summer pairing. The basil dressing is probably one of my most-used dressings, and I make it all summer long. It's tangy, fresh and creamy, thanks to the buttery goodness of the walnuts, which also provide skin-soothing omega-3 fatty acids. All the elements of this bowl can be made in advance, and they store well in the fridge for 2–3 days, making the perfect fast and flavoursome food fix on a sunny day.

SERVES 2

250g cherry tomatoes, cut in half
a drizzle of extra virgin olive oil
100g buckwheat grains, rinsed
    and drained
120g pitted olives (I love a mix of
    Kalamata and green), sliced
1 tbsp small capers
½ a red onion, finely chopped
1 x 400g tin of cannellini beans,
    drained and rinsed
a sprinkle of chilli flakes
    (optional)
a handful of parsley (about 10g),
    finely chopped
salt and pepper, to taste

FOR THE DRESSING:
4 tbsp extra virgin olive oil
1 tbsp lemon juice
20g walnuts
1 garlic clove
1 tsp Dijon mustard
½ tbsp nutritional yeast
a generous handful of basil
    leaves (10–15g)
salt and pepper, to taste

SERVE WITH:
1 avocado, peeled, stoned and
    sliced or chopped
a sprinkle of my Roasted Tamari
    Super-seed Mix (page 107)

Preheat the oven to 160°C/140°C fan/gas 3.

Put the tomatoes on a large baking tray, making sure there is space between them. Drizzle them with extra virgin olive oil, add a pinch each of salt and pepper, and gently toss them around so they get evenly coated. Roast in the oven for 35–40 minutes, until the tomatoes are soft and squishy but still holding their shape.

Meanwhile, put the buckwheat grains into a pan and cover them with plenty of salted boiling water (like you would do with pasta). Cook for 15–18 minutes, until the grains are soft but not mushy. Drain, then set to one side to cool down.

Make the dressing next. Put all the ingredients into a blender along with 2 tablespoons of water and blend until smooth. Set aside.

Put the sliced olives, capers, red onion, cannellini beans, chilli flakes (if using), chopped parsley and cooked buckwheat into a large bowl and stir to combine. Drizzle with a little extra virgin olive oil.

To serve, put the buckwheat and cannellini bean mix into your bowls and add the slow-roasted tomatoes and avocado. Divide the dressing between the two bowls and stir everything together. If you fancy an extra crunch, serve with a generous sprinkle of my Roasted Tamari Super-seed Mix.

TIP
If you are not a big fan of raw red onion you can substitute 3 or 4 finely chopped spring onions.

Cheesy Squash Millet with Miso Brussels Sprouts

Brussels sprouts, like broccoli and kale, are a member of the cruciferous vegetable family, which are kind of rockstars in the veg world for their incredible cancer-fighting properties. Brussels sprouts also contain a phytochemical called indole-3-carbinol that helps eliminate excess estrogen, helping to keep our hormones in balance. Getting the right balance of hormones is so important for skin health, as any imbalances can lead to acne and the acceleration of skin ageing. Sadly, Brussels sprouts are mostly only eaten during the festive holidays when actually, they are rocking all year round. I enjoy roasting them with a miso and maple dressing, which injects tons of flavour and a touch of sweetness to perfectly balance the natural bitterness of the sprouts. I serve them with a creamy squash millet, which makes this bowl comforting and really filling, the perfect easy dinner for cold nights.

SERVES 2

200g pumpkin or butternut squash, peeled and cut into cubes
2 tbsp nutritional yeast
½ tsp smoked paprika
1 tbsp lemon juice
100ml unsweetened plant milk (I have used oat)
1 tbsp olive oil, for frying
1 small white onion, finely chopped
2 garlic cloves, crushed
130g millet, rinsed
700ml vegetable stock
salt and pepper, to taste

FOR THE BRUSSELS SPROUTS:

3 tbsp olive oil
1 tbsp white miso paste
1 tsp wholegrain mustard
½ tbsp maple syrup
150g Brussels sprouts, trimmed and cut in half
salt and pepper, to taste

SERVE WITH:

a handful of fresh thyme leaves
a sprinkle of Roasted Tamari Super-seed Mix (page 107)

Steam or boil the squash until soft enough to be pierced with a fork. Drain and transfer it to a blender. Add the nutritional yeast, smoked paprika, lemon juice, plant milk and a generous pinch each of salt and pepper, and blend everything until smooth and creamy. Set aside.

Preheat the oven to 200°C/180°C fan/gas 6 and line a large baking tray with baking paper.

Put the oil into a deep frying pan on a medium heat and, once hot, add the chopped onion. Cook for 5–8 minutes, until it starts to caramelize. Add the crushed garlic and cook for another minute. Add the millet, stir to combine, then pour in the vegetable stock. Bring to the boil, then cover with the lid and cook on a low heat for 15–20 minutes, until the millet has absorbed all the liquid and it has the consistency of polenta.

In the meantime, cook the Brussels sprouts. Put the olive oil, miso paste, mustard and maple syrup into a large bowl and mix well until you have a paste. Add the Brussels sprouts and toss them around in the dressing until they are well coated. Spread them on the lined baking tray (making sure there is space between the sprouts so they will get crispier) and roast in the oven for 20–25 minutes, until golden brown.

Add the squash cream to the cooked millet and mix well. Turn the heat up for just a minute to make sure everything is hot. If your millet is looking a bit dry, add a dash of plant milk and keep cooking for another minute.

Serve the millet with the roasted Brussels sprouts on top. Sprinkle with thyme leaves and Roasted Tamari Super-seed Mix.

Green Goddess Bowl with Avocado & Macadamia Pesto

This is one of my go-to lunches when life gets busy. It takes only 20 minutes to make, it's packed with so much goodness and deliciousness, and it's guaranteed to keep me feeling full and energized until dinner time. I have used a mix of cruciferous vegetables for their incredible cancer-fighting benefits and antioxidants, minerals and vitamins for the skin. The avocado and macadamia pesto lifts and brings this dish together, making it super-scrumptious! Avocados are one of the healthiest sources of fats, and we do need fats to keep our skin supple and to fight inflammation. Avocado provides vitamin E, which is a powerful antioxidant that keeps skin hydrated, and vitamins B such as niacin, which helps to reduce redness and inflammation in the skin. To make this recipe even quicker, cook the quinoa in advance and you will have a delicious and nourishing bowl in absolutely no time.

SERVES 2

100g quinoa
120g tenderstem broccoli, roughly chopped
6–7 Brussels sprouts, trimmed and thinly sliced
2 large handfuls of chopped kale (50–60g)
1 tbsp white miso paste
100g frozen peas

FOR THE PESTO:
1 ripe avocado, peeled, stoned and roughly chopped
30g basil leaves
50g macadamia nuts (if you can't find them, cashews are great too)
3 tbsp extra virgin olive oil
juice of ½ a lemon
1 garlic clove
½ tbsp nutritional yeast
a generous pinch of salt

SERVE WITH:
a drizzle of good quality extra virgin olive oil
a twist of black pepper
lemon slices

Cook the quinoa according to the packet instructions.

In the meantime, make the pesto by simply putting all the ingredients into a food processor or a blender and blending until smooth and creamy. Leave to one side.

Put a drizzle of olive oil into a frying pan on a medium heat. Add the chopped tenderstem broccoli, Brussels sprouts and kale. Cook for 5 minutes, until the greens start to soften.

Mix the white miso paste in a small bowl with a little bit of water to dissolve any lumps. Pour the miso over the greens and add the frozen peas. Stir everything to combine and cook for another couple of minutes.

Assemble your bowls by putting some cooked quinoa at the bottom of each bowl, followed by the stir-fried greens, and top each bowl with a generous dollop of the avocado and macadamia pesto. Drizzle with oil, grind over a twist of pepper and serve with lemon slices.

Crispy Tempeh & Kale Caesar Bowl

I am a big believer that salads don't have to be boring, and this take on the classic Caesar salad can really prove it. What makes this salad so spectacular is the creamy and silky sunflower seed dressing, which also makes the kale much softer and more succulent. Sunflower seeds are brimming with essential fatty acids like linoleic, oleic and palmitic acid. To make this salad more filling I have added chickpeas and tempeh, both great sources of protein, fibre and calcium, essential for strong and healthy nails. The smoky chickpeas and crispy tempeh work so well in contrast with the creamy dressing and really make this salad fizz with flavour. Although this bowl is glorious as it is, I would highly recommend you to generously sprinkle over my Cheesy Walnut & Hemp Parm (page 106). Not only does it add a delicious nutty texture, it also provides a good amount of omega-3 fatty acids, vitamin B, vitamin E and antioxidants, which help in the battle against free radicals and premature ageing.

SERVES 2

½ x 400g tin of chickpeas, drained and rinsed (use the other half tin to make my Chickpea Chocolate Smoothie, page 191)
100g tempeh, crumbled
2 tbsp tamari sauce
1 tbsp maple syrup
1 tsp vegan-friendly Worcestershire sauce
½ tsp smoked paprika
1 tbsp olive oil
150g curly kale, de stemmed and finely chopped
1 head of romaine lettuce, chopped
150g cherry tomatoes, cut in halves
a generous sprinkle of my Cheesy Walnut & Hemp Parm (page 106), to serve

FOR THE DRESSING:

100g sunflower seeds, soaked in boiling water for 30 minutes, then drained
2 garlic cloves
1 tbsp nutritional yeast
1 tsp Dijon mustard
juice of 1 lemon
1 tbsp extra virgin olive oil
salt and pepper, to taste

Preheat the oven to 200°C/180°C fan/gas 6 and line a baking tray with baking paper.

Put the chickpeas and crumbled tempeh into a bowl together with the tamari sauce, maple syrup, Worcestershire sauce, smoked paprika and olive oil. Mix everything together and transfer it to the lined baking tray. Bake in the oven for 30 minutes, until the chickpeas and tempeh are crispy around the edges.

To make the dressing, simply put all the ingredients into a blender along with 100ml of cold water. Blend until creamy and smooth. Pour the dressing over the chopped kale and, using your hands, massage it into the kale until you feel the leaves start to wilt. Add the chopped romaine lettuce and the cherry tomatoes and mix everything together.

To serve, use the kale salad as the base of your bowls, add the roasted chickpeas and tempeh on top, and finish it off with a generous sprinkle of my Walnut & Hemp Parm.

Golden Tofu Curry Bowl

Looking for a curry in a hurry? Well, this one is for you. It's the kind of bowl that I make when I am short of time but I still want something yummy, nourishing and filling. To make this recipe even speedier, I often use leftover or pre-cooked rice, but other quick-cooking grains like quinoa will work too.

Bird's-eye chillies are undoubtedly fiery. I swear my sinuses clear and my nostrils breathe easier after I eat them! Chillies are very high in antioxidant carotenoids, which are linked to numerous health benefits. They are bursting with vitamin C, which helps boost collagen production for healthy, plump skin. Fiery chillies, fresh garlic and ginger are a holy trinity for the immune system with their anti-inflammatory properties. From a beauty point of view, both ginger and garlic are truly your skin's best friends. Ginger and its phytochemical gingerol may help to suppress the cell-ageing mechanism. Similarly, garlic contains allicin, a sulphurous phytochemical that helps to protect the skin from UV damage and premature ageing.

SERVES 2

100g brown basmati rice, rinsed
280–300g firm/extra firm tofu
2 tbsp melted coconut oil
200g purple sprouting broccoli or tenderstem, trimmed
2 shallots, finely chopped
2 garlic cloves, crushed
1 tbsp grated ginger
2 red bird's-eye chillies, finely chopped
1 tbsp curry powder
1 tsp ground turmeric
1 x 400ml tin of coconut milk
2 tsp coconut sugar
juice of ½ a lime
1 tbsp tamari sauce

SERVE WITH:
a sprinkle of chopped fresh coriander
lime wedges

Put the rinsed rice into a large pot and cover it with plenty of boiling water. Cook on a medium heat until the rice is cooked, about 25–30 minutes. Drain and leave to one side.

While the rice is cooking, wrap the tofu in a clean tea towel and place it on a plate. Cover it with something heavy, like a cast-iron pan or a ceramic pot, and leave it for 5–10 minutes so the majority of the liquid can drain out. Slice the tofu into cubes.

Put 1 tablespoon of the coconut oil into a large pan on a medium heat. Once piping hot, add the tofu cubes and fry for 3–4 minutes on each side, until golden brown all over. Remove the tofu from the pan and transfer to a plate. Add the purple sprouting broccoli to the same pan and cook for about 5 minutes, until it is slightly charred around the edges. Using a pair of tongs or two forks, remove the broccoli from the pan and transfer it to the plate, together with the tofu.

Add the remaining tablespoon of coconut oil to the pan, together with the chopped shallots. Stir-fry for 5 minutes, until the shallots are translucent and slightly caramelized. Add the garlic, ginger and chillies and cook for 2 more minutes. Keep stirring, as garlic and ginger can burn very easily. Add the curry powder and turmeric and stir to combine. Add the coconut milk and coconut sugar and mix everything together.

Add the tofu and broccoli to the pan and cook on a simmer for 5 minutes.

Season with the lime juice and tamari sauce. Stir and serve with chopped fresh coriander, lime wedges and the cooked rice.

Trio of Sprinkles

These three supercharged nut and seed sprinkles are a staple in my kitchen. They can instantly inject flavour, texture, and of course lots of skin vitality to virtually any meal. Any of these sprinkles will transform your regular avocado toast, soups, salads or even a simple baked potato into something unexpectedly delectable.

MAKES A 250ML JAR

60g almonds
60g hazelnuts
4 tbsp sesame seeds
2 tbsp coriander seeds
2 tbsp cumin seeds
2 tbsp fennel seeds
1½ tsp sea salt
a twist of black pepper
1 tbsp chilli flakes (optional)

ALMOND & HAZELNUT DUKKAH

Freshly made dukkah is a delight. It's my new favourite seasoning and lends irresistibly nutty, subtly spiced nuances to everything it touches. The natural sweetness of the hazelnut and almonds goes so well with the warm, refreshing notes of coriander, cumin and fennel – a great aid for digestion. The supreme sprinkle is excellent for enhancing any dish with some skin-nourishing vitamin E and healthy fats, for example my Almond Butter & Shiitake Mushroom Bowl (page 85) or my Spicy Roots & Millet Bowl (page 89).

Preheat the oven to 170°C/150°C fan/gas 3.

Put the almonds and hazelnuts on a baking tray and bake in the oven for 10 minutes. Add the sesame seeds, coriander, cumin and fennel seeds, then put the tray back into the oven for a final 10 minutes.

Transfer the nuts and seeds to a food processor together with the salt, black pepper and chilli flakes (if using), and pulse a few times until you have a crumbly kind of consistency. Transfer to a clean jar or airtight container and store in the fridge (for optimum freshness) for up to 3–4 weeks.

MAKES A 250ML JAR

100g walnuts
50g hemp seeds
4 tbsp nutritional yeast
1 tbsp white miso paste
a twist of black pepper

CHEESY WALNUT & HEMP PARM

When I first cut out dairy, Parmesan was definitely one of the things I missed the most until I started making my plant-powered version. I am not saying that this sprinkle tastes exactly like Parmesan cheese, but I have to say it's incredibly cheesy and oh so addictive. The walnut and hemp, together with the nutritional yeast and miso paste, create the most deliciously intense umami combo and add lots of skin-strengthening omega-3 fatty acids. I warn you, you will want to sprinkle it on top of everything, not just pasta! I love it sprinkled on top of my Crispy Tempeh & Kale Caesar Bowl (page 101) for an extra injection of flavour and texture.

Preheat the oven to 170°C/150°C fan/gas 3.

Put the walnuts on a baking tray and bake in the oven for 10 minutes. Remove and allow to cool down completely. Put the walnuts into a food processor with the rest of the ingredients, and blitz to a crumbly consistency. Transfer to a clean jar or airtight container, and store in the fridge (for optimum freshness) for up to 3–4 weeks.

70g sunflower seeds
70g pumpkin seeds
40g sesame seeds
2 tbsp nutritional yeast
2 tsp dried rosemary
1 tsp smoked paprika
2 tbsp tamari sauce
1 tbsp olive oil

ROASTED TAMARI SUPER-SEED MIX

This seed mix is super-versatile. It can be used as a crispy salad topping, a soup garnish or an all-purpose seasoning that will heighten the final taste and add texture. It also adds extra nutrients to your plate, such as manganese and calcium from sesame seeds, vitamin E from sunflower seeds and zinc from the pumpkin seeds, to mention just a few. I particularly adore it sprinkled on top of my Asparagus & Pea Soup (page 152) or my Parsnip, Apple & Leek Soup (page 149) for a crunchy bite.

Preheat the oven to 120°C/100°C fan/gas ½ and line a large baking tray with parchment paper.

Put the sunflower, pumpkin and sesame seeds into a large bowl. Add the nutritional yeast, dried rosemary and smoked paprika and mix. Add the tamari sauce and olive oil, and mix everything until the seeds are well coated with the seasoning.

Spread the seed mixture on the lined baking tray and bake in the oven for 30 minutes. Remove and let the seeds cool down completely, then transfer them to a clean jar or container. Store in the fridge (for optimum freshness) for up to 3–4 weeks.

Soulful Pasta

My wonderful online community has often called me the 'Pasta Queen', a title which has always made me very proud. During the 6 years that I have spent creating recipes online, my pasta dishes have always been my most popular and most-loved recipes, and many of my followers have made them countless times. Pasta sparks so much love and joy in most of us. In all honesty, I could probably write a whole book just about pasta – maybe that's an idea for another time!

"Pasta for me will always represent pleasure, bliss and ease. It's my ultimate comfort food."

Having grown up in Italy, pasta always brings back nostalgic memories. I remember my mum making us her quick tomato pasta during busy school nights and having fresh filled pasta like tortellini or tortelloni on Sunday for lunch. Both my grandmas would often do a fresh pasta 'marathon'. It would usually happen during the weekend, and they would call my mum and my aunties round to make lasagne or fresh pasta to freeze. It truly was a family affair. They would all sit around the table in a very methodical production system, and us little ones would try to sneak off with some of the delicious fillings without getting caught. I remember watching transfixed as my grandma would roll fresh pasta dough, shaping small pieces into tortellini, the iconic fresh pasta from Bologna. These tortellini would then be frozen, to be served during celebrations like Christmas or Easter. Every Italian nonna has her own special recipes, which have probably been passed down for generations. If you travel across Italy you will find hundreds of different recipes, even for something super-simple like pasta al pomodoro (pasta with tomato sauce). Pasta in Italy is a matter of national pride and cohesion, but what I've come to realize is that it's a food that transcends borders and is enjoyed in all corners of the world.

Pasta for me will always represent pleasure, bliss and ease. It's my ultimate comfort food, and always feels like a cosy blanket. Sadly, it gets a bad rep and is often pictured as something that's unhealthy or fattening.

My Italian soul always cries on the inside when I read or hear such absurdities. Pasta is really not the enemy, especially when there are so many more wholesome varieties available to choose from. As always, I like to keep it as whole and unrefined as possible, so I love using brown rice, quinoa or chickpea pasta. I find brown rice and quinoa pastas the closest in terms of texture when compared to white wheat pasta. Chickpea and yellow pea pastas are great too, especially as they bring in a good dose of plant-based protein and fibre. Pasta in my eyes is also the original 'fast food', quick and easy. Apart from my Cashew Ricotta Veggie Lasagna recipe, which takes a bit longer, all the recipes in this chapter take under 30 minutes to whizz up, making them the perfect midweek suppers. My favourite speedy recipes are my Pea & Broccoli Pasta and my Caponata Chickpea Pasta. Both are packed with veg and ready in no time. In summer, I adore my Lemon & Tahini Courgette Pasta, my Pasta alla Trapanese and my Gremolata Orecchiette with Roasted Tomatoes. They're all bursting with vibrant flavours and seasonal produce.

Most of the pasta sauces in this chapter can be made in advance and stored in the fridge for 2 to 3 days, and some of them are also suitable for freezing.

Caponata Chickpea Pasta

Caponata is a quintessential Sicilian dish of aubergine, tomato, raisins and capers, usually served with toasted ciabatta bread. I made countless different versions of this recipe, especially during the summer months when my dad's garden was overflowing with an abundance of ripe produce.

I particularly love this more filling version with chickpeas and pasta. It's one of my go-to summer dinners because it's super-easy and quick to make. It's packed with antioxidant-rich vegetables and a good amount of protein and fibre from the chickpeas that will help to keep your skin nourished and protected from free radicals. Any leftover caponata will store well in the fridge for few days and it's delicious on its own.

SERVES 4

1 medium aubergine, cut into small cubes
3 tbsp extra virgin olive oil
1 medium white onion, finely chopped
3 garlic cloves, crushed
1 x 400g tin of chopped tomatoes
200g cherry tomatoes, cut in halves
1 tbsp small capers
2 tbsp raisins
½ x 400g tin of chickpeas, drained and rinsed
a bunch of fresh basil (20–30g), roughly chopped + extra for serving
360g pasta of your choice (I have used conchiglie)
salt and pepper, to taste

Preheat the oven to 200°C/180°C fan/gas 6.

Put the chopped aubergine on a large baking tray. Drizzle with 2 tablespoons of the olive oil and sprinkle with a generous pinch each of salt and pepper. Toss the aubergine cubes around so they are evenly coated. Roast in the oven for 20 minutes, until soft.

Heat the remaining olive oil in a large pan on a medium heat and cook the onion for 8–10 minutes, until it starts to caramelize. Add the crushed garlic and cook for another 2 minutes. Make sure you keep stirring to prevent burning. Add the tinned tomatoes, cherry tomatoes, capers, raisins and drained chickpeas. Season with salt and pepper and cook on a simmer for 20 minutes. Remove the aubergine cubes from the oven and add them to the tomato sauce, together with the chopped basil. Stir everything to combine and cook for another 10 minutes.

Cook the pasta according to the packet instructions. Drain, but make sure you reserve a couple of tablespoons of the pasta cooking water. Add the pasta water to the tomato sauce to loosen it. Add the pasta to the pan with the tomato sauce and mix everything together.

Serve with extra basil leaves.

Pea & Broccoli Pasta

This recipe is a perfect example of how much goodness you can sneak into a bowl of pasta. It's also the perfect recipe to up your green intake in a completely fuss-free and delicious way. The broccoli, pea and cashew sauce is creamy, silky, and with lots of fresh notes from the peas and lemon is beautifully balanced by the intense umami flavours of the miso paste and nutritional yeast. Broccoli is inexpensive, widely available and unbelievably nutrient-dense. It is a wonderful source of two of my favourite beauty vitamins, A and C, and also contains lutein, which helps protect your skin from oxidative damage. After a long day at work, this is effortlessly easy, comforting and still crammed with veg.

SERVES 2

1 tbsp olive oil, for cooking
1 shallot, finely chopped
½ a head of broccoli, florets only, chopped finely
2 garlic cloves, crushed
½ tbsp white miso paste
200ml unsweetened oat milk
180g frozen peas
40g raw cashews, soaked in boiling water for 30 minutes
juice of ½ a lemon
1 tbsp nutritional yeast
180g of your favourite pasta (for this recipe I love spaghetti)
a handful of baby spinach (optional)
extra virgin olive oil, for drizzling

Put the olive oil into a frying pan on a medium heat and add the chopped shallot. Cook for 5–8 minutes, until the shallot starts to caramelize. Add the chopped broccoli and crushed garlic, stir everything together and cook for 1–2 minutes, until the garlic is fragrant.

Add the miso paste and 100ml of the oat milk, cover with a lid and cook for around 8 minutes, until the broccoli has softened. Add about 100g of the frozen peas, then stir everything together and cook for a final 5 minutes.

Transfer everything to a blender and add the remaining oat milk, the soaked and drained cashews, lemon juice and nutritional yeast. Blend until smooth and creamy. Set aside.

Cook the pasta according to the packet instructions. Two minutes before it is ready, add the remaining frozen peas to the pan. Drain the pasta and peas but make sure you reserve 5 tablespoons of the cooking water. Add the cooking water to the broccoli sauce and mix. Put the pasta back into the pan and drizzle with a little extra virgin olive oil. If using, stir through the baby spinach. Pour the sauce into the pasta and stir until well combined.

Pulled Mushroom Pasta

This is my favourite rapid pasta when I want something really comforting and full of flavour. The mix of oyster and porcini mushrooms together with the miso and oat milk creates an incredibly rich and creamy sauce. Apart from their immune-supporting benefits, oyster mushrooms boast incredible antioxidants to help protect your skin from oxidative stress and free radicals. If you would like to add more veg to this recipe, simply stir in some baby spinach when mixing the pasta with the mushroom sauce.

SERVES 2

15g dried porcini mushrooms
100g oyster mushrooms
1 tbsp olive oil
180g of the pasta of your choice
    (I love tagliatelle for this recipe)
2 large garlic cloves, crushed
½ tbsp tamari sauce
1 tbsp white miso paste
50ml oat milk
1 tsp Dijon mustard
1 tbsp nutritional yeast
a handful of fresh parsley (about
    10g), finely chopped

SERVE WITH:
a twist of black pepper
a drizzle of extra virgin olive oil

Put the dried porcini mushrooms into a heatproof bowl and cover with plenty of boiling water. Let them soak for 20 minutes, until they have softened. Drain and chop them finely but make sure you keep the soaking water.

Using your hands, 'pull' the oyster mushrooms into thin strips. Put the olive oil into a large frying pan on a medium heat and, when it's hot, add the pulled oyster mushrooms. Cook for 5 minutes, until golden brown around the edges.

Start cooking the pasta according to the packet instructions. Add the crushed garlic to the mushrooms and stir continuously for 1–2 minutes. Add the soaked porcini mushrooms and combine everything together. Add the tamari sauce and miso paste, stir everything together and cook for a couple more minutes. Add the oat milk, Dijon mustard, nutritional yeast and 2 tablespoons of the porcini soaking water. Stir everything together and turn down to a low heat. Cook for a final 5–7 minutes, until the sauce has thickened up slightly.

Drain the pasta, reserving about ½ a cup of the cooking water. Add the pasta to the pan of mushrooms together with the chopped parsley and the pasta cooking water. Stir everything together for 1 minute, then serve with a twist of black pepper and a drizzle of extra virgin olive oil.

Cacio e Pepe Pasta with Smoky Mushrooms

Before I transitioned to a plant-based diet, cacio e pepe (cacio cheese and pepper) pasta was probably my idea of heaven on a plate. I still remember being in Rome in this tiny trattoria slurping creamy cacio e pepe bucatini thinking: 'I could never give up cheese.' Fast forward a few years and I am so happy I have managed to recreate the creaminess, taste and texture of cacio e pepe sauce without using dairy and using only natural ingredients. Silken tofu is ideal for this recipe, because when it is blended with nutritional yeast, miso paste and pasta water it creates a luscious, silky cheesy sauce. Tofu is also a wonderful source of plant-based protein that enhances your skin's elasticity, keeping it youthful. The addition of the smoky mushrooms ramps up the flavour, adds extra texture and brings a good dose of beauty-boosting antioxidants and selenium.

SERVES 2

300g silken tofu, drained
4 tbsp nutritional yeast
1½ tbsp lemon juice
1 tsp garlic powder
1 tbsp white miso paste
a generous pinch each of salt and pepper + extra pepper to serve
180g pasta of your choice (for this recipe I love tagliatelle or spaghetti)

FOR THE SMOKY MUSHROOMS:

1 tbsp tamari sauce
1 tbsp olive oil
1 tsp maple syrup
1 tsp tomato purée
½ tsp smoked paprika
a twist of black pepper
300g chestnut mushrooms, sliced

Preheat the oven to 200°C/180°C fan/gas 6 and line a baking tray with parchment paper.

In a bowl, mix the tamari sauce, olive oil, maple syrup, tomato purée, smoked paprika and black pepper. Add the sliced mushrooms, then give everything a good mix so the mushrooms get nicely coated with the sauce.

Spread the mushrooms on the lined tray and bake them in the oven for 20–25 minutes, until all the water has evaporated and the mushrooms are slightly crispy around the edges.

In the meantime, put the silken tofu, nutritional yeast, lemon juice, garlic powder, miso paste, salt and pepper into a blender and blend until fairly smooth. Add a dash of water if your blender is struggling. Leave the mixture in the blender while you cook the pasta.

Cook the pasta according to the packet instructions. Remove 4 tablespoons of the cooking water and add to the tofu mixture in the blender. Blend again until smooth and creamy. Drain the pasta, put it back in the pan, and pour in the creamy tofu sauce. Mix everything together and add the smoky mushrooms (making sure to reserve some to sprinkle on top). Serve with a generous twist of black pepper.

Pasta alla Trapanese

Pesto alla Trapanese is Sicily's answer to Liguria's more famous basil pesto. I first had it when I visited Sicily and it made an instant impression on me. It's fresh, light and spectacular in the summer months, when our home-grown tomatoes are ripe and juicy. It's one of those beautifully simple Italian recipes that take no time at all to make and yet it is incredibly scrumptious. The almonds pack this dish with some powerful beauty-boosting vitamin E and the tomatoes bring in vitamin C and antioxidants, perfect for boosting collagen for plumper and bouncier skin. The tomatoes are the star of the show here, as they add a delicious fruity flavour, so make sure you buy the ripest and reddest you can find. Or have a go at growing them yourself – it's easy, and the flavour of home-grown tomatoes can't be beaten.

SERVES 2

50g almonds
30g fresh basil + extra for
    sprinkling on top
1 garlic clove
juice of ½ a lemon
3 tbsp extra virgin olive oil
    + extra for drizzling
180g pasta of your choice
    (I love bucatini or spaghetti
    for this recipe)
300g vine tomatoes
salt and pepper, to taste

Preheat the oven to 220°C/200°C fan/gas 7.

Put the almonds on a baking tray and roast them in the oven for 10 minutes. Remove and let them cool down.

Put the roasted almonds into a food processor with the basil, garlic, lemon juice, extra virgin olive oil, and a pinch each of salt and pepper and blitz until you have a creamy consistency.

Cook the pasta according to the packet instructions. In the meantime, grate the tomatoes using the largest hole of the grater. Reserve the pulp and discard the skins.

Once the pasta is cooked, drain it but make sure you save a couple of tablespoons of the cooking water. Add the cooking water to the almond pesto and stir to combine. Mix the pesto with the pasta and the tomato pulp. Serve with a generous drizzle of extra virgin olive oil and some basil leaves.

Cashew Ricotta Veggie Lasagne

Growing up in Italy we would always have lasagne for Sunday lunch. It's probably one of my favourite comfort food recipes. This is my plant-based version of my mum's traditional lasagne alla Bolognese. Instead of the classic béchamel sauce, I have made a cashew-tofu ricotta-style cheese that is just so creamy and full of flavour. Although it tastes very indulgent, it is crammed with vegetables, lots of fibre and protein and a good dose of skin-loving zinc, thanks to the cashews. Try serving it with a big green salad or a tray of roasted greens on the side.

SERVES 6

1 medium onion, chopped
1 medium carrot, chopped
1 stick of celery, chopped
olive oil, for cooking
a few sprigs of fresh thyme + extra
    for sprinkling on top
1 tsp smoked paprika
250g chestnut mushrooms
3 garlic cloves, crushed
1 tbsp brown miso paste
1 tbsp tamari sauce
1 x 400g tin of chopped tomatoes
2 tbsp tomato purée
250g cooked Puy or French lentils
700ml veggie stock
200g baby spinach
10–12 lasagne sheets (I have used
    brown rice pasta sheets)

FOR THE CASHEW RICOTTA:

200g raw cashews, soaked in
    boiling water for 30 minutes,
    then drained
300g firm tofu
6 tbsp nutritional yeast
1 tsp Dijon mustard
1½ tbsp white miso paste
2 tbsp apple cider vinegar
2 tbsp lemon juice
a generous twist of black pepper
salt, to taste

Put the onion, carrot and celery into a food processor and pulse for a few seconds until they are finely chopped. Put a drizzle of olive oil into a large pan on a medium heat. Add the finely chopped vegetables, together with the thyme sprigs and smoked paprika. Cook for 5–8 minutes, until they start to caramelize.

In the meantime, put the mushrooms into the food processor (no need to wash) and blitz until you have a fairly fine mixture. Add the mushrooms and crushed garlic to the pan of vegetables and cook for another 5–8 minutes, until all the liquid has evaporated. Add the miso paste, tamari sauce, tinned tomatoes, tomato purée and lentils and stir to combine. Pour in the veggie stock, bring everything to the boil, then turn down to a simmer and cook for 30–35 minutes, until you have a rich and thick sauce. Remove from the heat and set aside.

While your ragù is cooking, make the cashew ricotta. Simply put all the ingredients into a food processor and blitz until you have a creamy mixture. Taste and adjust for seasoning. Put the baby spinach into a pan on a medium heat with a drizzle of olive oil and cook for 5–7 minutes, until the spinach leaves start to wilt. Remove from the heat.

Preheat the oven to 200°C/180°C fan/gas 6. Start by spreading a layer of lentil ragù at the bottom of your oven dish (mine is 30 x 20cm). Layer the lasagne sheets on top. Make sure there are no gaps. If you need to, break up a lasagne sheet to fill up the empty spaces. Layer some more ragù on top. Dot around about half the cashew ricotta and baby spinach. Cover with another layer of lasagne sheets. Add more ragù on top and more of the cashew ricotta, but make sure you have some left for the final layer. Add the remaining spinach. Cover with more lasagne sheets and spread the remaining ragù on top, followed by the rest of the ricotta. Sprinkle with thyme sprigs.

Cover the dish with kitchen foil and bake in the oven for 45 minutes, then take off the foil and bake for another 15 minutes. Leave to stand for 10 minutes before serving.

Silky Sweet Potato Pasta

Sometimes you just need a big bowl of pasta, and this is my absolute favourite for those days. The creamy sweet potato and tofu sauce with nutritional yeast creates a slightly cheesy flavour, making it feel almost like a plant-based style mac 'n' cheese. Not only is this pasta highly addictive, but thanks to the sweet potato it gives you a generous hit of beautifying vitamin A, which is so powerful in healing and smoothing the skin and also protecting against UV rays. The creamy sauce can be made in advance and stored in the fridge for 2 or 3 days, perfect for a healthy and comforting meal in no time.

SERVES 4

1 medium sweet potato (around 500g), peeled and chopped into pieces
a drizzle of olive oil, for roasting
300g silken tofu, drained
2 tbsp nutritional yeast
1 tsp onion powder
1 tsp garlic powder
1 tsp smoked paprika
½ tsp ground turmeric
1 tbsp lemon juice
1 tsp Dijon mustard
360g pasta of your choice (I have used penne)
salt and pepper, to taste

Preheat the oven to 200°C/180°C fan/gas 6. Put the chopped sweet potato on a large baking tray, drizzle with olive oil and sprinkle with salt and pepper. Roast in the oven for 30–35 minutes, until the sweet potato is cooked.

Remove from the oven and transfer to a blender together with the silken tofu, nutritional yeast, onion powder, garlic powder, smoked paprika, turmeric, lemon juice and Dijon mustard. Blend until fairly smooth. Taste and adjust the salt and pepper.

Cook the pasta according to the packet instructions. Just before draining, remove 4–5 tablespoons of the cooking water and add to the blender. Blend the sweet potato sauce again until super-silky.

Drain the pasta and mix it with the sauce. Serve with a twist of black pepper.

Dhal Pita

The first time I had dhal pita, my Italian heart sang with joy. Spicy curried lentils with silky pasta (pita) cooked in it, what more can you ask for? Traditionally the dough for the pita is made from scratch, but for ease in this recipe I have used brown rice lasagne sheets, which actually work perfectly well. Lentils are often overlooked, even though they're an inexpensive way of getting a wide range of nutrients. They're packed with B vitamins, magnesium, zinc and potassium. Lentils are also high in fibre, which supports regular bowel movements and the growth of healthy gut bacteria. Split red lentils take very little time to cook, and they soak up any flavour you add to them. This bowl of joy is hearty, warming, and comes together in just over 30 minutes, making it the perfect midweek dinner.

SERVES 2

1 tbsp melted coconut oil, for cooking
2 shallots, finely chopped
1 red chilli, chopped
3 garlic cloves, crushed
1 tbsp grated ginger
1 tsp ground turmeric
1 tbsp curry powder
200g split red lentils, rinsed
½ x 400ml tin of full-fat coconut milk
1 litre veggie stock
100g brown rice lasagne sheets, broken into large pieces
a handful of baby spinach (optional)
salt and pepper, to taste

SERVE WITH:
chopped fresh coriander
a pinch of chilli flakes (optional)
handful of toasted flaked coconut

Put the oil into a large pan on a medium heat. Once hot, add the chopped shallots and chilli and cook for 5–8 minutes, until the shallots start to caramelize. Add the crushed garlic, ginger, turmeric and curry powder. Stir to combine and cook for another minute. Add the rinsed lentils and coconut milk and mix everything together. Pour in the veggie stock and turn the heat down to a simmer. Cook the dhal for around 20 minutes, until the lentils have gone mushy.

Add the broken lasagne sheets and cook for another 10 minutes. Make sure you keep stirring while they cook, as they tend to stick to the bottom of the pan and to each other. Add the baby spinach (if using) and mix everything together until the spinach leaves have wilted. Serve with chopped coriander, some chilli flakes for extra heat (if using), and a sprinkle of toasted flaked coconut.

TIP
The dhal stores well in the fridge for a few days and is suitable for freezing too. Just cook fresh lasagne sheets and add them to the heated-up dhal to serve.

Sunflower Ragù Rigatoni

This pasta dish is a staple in our house. Even my carnivore boyfriend loves it, and we make it at least once a week because it's so simple, really flavourful, and any leftover sauce can be stashed away in the freezer for another day. Sunflower seeds are often overlooked, but they are a powerhouse of skin nutrition. They are brimming with selenium, important for cell repair, and vitamin E, which is vital in the production of collagen and elastin. They are also packed with antioxidants to fight oxidative stress, resulting in younger-looking skin. Combine the earthy mushrooms, herbs and miso paste to create a rich and hearty sauce.

SERVES 4

20g dried porcini mushrooms, roughly chopped
100g sunflower seeds
1 medium white onion, roughly chopped
1 carrot, roughly chopped
1 stick of celery, roughly chopped
1 tbsp olive oil, for cooking
300g chestnut mushrooms
3 garlic cloves, crushed
1 x 400g tin of chopped tomatoes
1 tbsp tomato purée
1 tsp dried thyme
1 tsp dried rosemary
1 tbsp brown miso paste
360g pasta of your choice (I love rigatoni for this recipe)
salt and pepper, to taste
a sprinkle of chopped fresh parsley, to serve

Put the porcini mushrooms into a large heatproof bowl and cover them with 250ml of boiling water. Let them soak for 10–15 minutes while you get on with the rest of the prep.

Put the sunflower seeds into a food processor and pulse a few times until you have a crumbly kind of texture. Transfer to a dry frying pan on a medium heat and toast for about 5 minutes. Remove the pan from the heat and leave to one side.

Add the onion, carrot and celery to the food processor and blitz until they are finely chopped.

Put the oil into a large pan and, when it's hot, add the onion mixture with a pinch of salt and cook on a medium heat for 5–8 minutes, until the vegetables start to soften and caramelize.

Add the mushrooms to the food processor and blitz again until you have a fine mixture. Add the blitzed mushrooms and crushed garlic to the pan of vegetables. Cook for 10–15 minutes, until the water from the mushrooms has evaporated.

Add in the tinned tomatoes, tomato purée, thyme, rosemary, miso paste and the soaked porcini with their water. Stir to combine, then keep cooking at a simmer for 20–25 minutes. You want a thick and rich sauce with no excess liquid. Add the toasted sunflower seeds and cook for a final 5 minutes.

Cook the pasta according to the packet instructions, then drain and stir into the ragù. Serve with a sprinkle of chopped parsley.

Gremolata Orecchiette with Roasted Tomatoes

Gremolata is a zesty Italian herb sauce traditionally served with meat. I am a big fan of its tanginess and freshness, and over the years I've developed my own version which I generally serve with pasta for a quick summertime dinner. The main ingredient in gremolata is parsley, which is loaded with collagen-boosting vitamin C and vitamin K. I love cashews for creaminess and for some breakout-fighting zinc. This pasta can either be enjoyed hot or cold, so it's another lunch-box hero. The slow-roasted tomatoes add a gorgeous juicy sweetness and they elevate the whole dish, so please don't skip them!

SERVES 4

200g cherry tomatoes, sliced in half
2 tbsp extra virgin olive oil + extra for roasting the tomatoes
30g fresh parsley + extra for serving
30g cashews
zest and juice of ½ a lemon (buy organic and unwaxed if you can)
2 garlic cloves, crushed
360g pasta of your choice (I love orecchiette for this recipe)
50g pitted green olives, roughly chopped
2 tbsp small capers
salt and pepper, to taste

Preheat the oven to 170°C/150°C fan/gas 3.

Put the tomatoes into a large baking tray, cut sides facing upwards. Drizzle with some olive oil and a generous pinch each of salt and pepper, and roast in the oven for 30 minutes.

Meanwhile, make the gremolata. Put the parsley, cashews, lemon zest and juice, garlic, olive oil and a generous pinch of salt into a food processor and blitz until fairly smooth.

Cook the pasta according to the packet instructions. If you are having it as a cold salad, drain it, rinse it under cold water, then transfer it to a bowl and mix it with the gremolata, roasted tomatoes, chopped olives and capers.

If you are having it hot, drain the pasta but make sure you reserve 2 tablespoons of the cooking water. Put the pasta back into the pan and add the gremolata, chopped olives and capers and the pasta cooking water. Mix everything together and serve topped with the roasted tomatoes, with an extra sprinkle of parsley.

Lemon & Tahini Courgette Pasta

The first time I made this recipe was on a warm Italian summer evening. My dad's garden was brimming with courgettes and I was scraping my brain for a dinner idea which didn't require much effort or too many ingredients. As with most improvised recipes, this humble pasta turned out better than I thought. The creamy and earthy tahini mixed with the zesty lemon juice, fresh herbs and umami miso paste makes the most luscious and delicious sauce. I know it might sound odd to add tahini to pasta but trust me, it works. Tahini is also rich in beauty vitamins like thiamine and niacin. These two B vitamins have essential roles when it comes to hydrating and repairing our skin. The Walnut & Hemp Parm adds a delicious cheesy flavour and also brings in some beneficial omega-3 fatty acids, which help to lower skin inflammation (resulting in fewer breakouts) and strengthen the skin's barrier. I love the utter simplicity of this recipe – simple ingredients, maximum flavour.

SERVES 2

1 tsp white miso paste

2 tbsp runny tahini

zest and juice of 1 lemon (buy organic and unwaxed if you can)

2 tbsp nutritional yeast

1 tsp Dijon mustard

2 tbsp extra virgin olive oil + extra for drizzling on top

1 banana shallot or 2 round ones, finely chopped

3 large garlic cloves, crushed

1 courgette, cut into matchsticks

180g pasta of your choice (I love spaghetti for this recipe)

a small handful of parsley (around 10g), chopped

a bunch of fresh basil (20–30g), chopped

2 tbsp small capers

salt and pepper, to taste

a sprinkle of my Cheesy Walnut & Hemp Parm (page 106), to serve

In a bowl, mix together the miso paste, tahini, lemon zest and juice, nutritional yeast and Dijon mustard. Leave to one side.

Put 2 tablespoons of olive oil into a large pan on a medium heat. Add the chopped shallot and cook for 5–8 minutes, until it starts to caramelize. Add the garlic and cook for another couple of minutes.

Add the chopped courgette with a generous pinch of salt and cook on a medium heat for 5–8 minutes, until the courgette starts to soften.

Cook the pasta according to the packet instructions. When it's al dente, remove ½ a cup of the cooking water and drain the pasta. Add the pasta to the pan of vegetables and add the tahini mixture, chopped parsley, basil, capers and the reserved cooking water. On a medium heat, mix the pasta with the sauce and fresh herbs until it's well coated.

Serve the pasta with my Cheesy Walnut & Hemp Parm, a drizzle of extra virgin olive oil and a twist of black pepper.

Nourishing
Soups
& Stews

Hearty and crammed with gratifying
goodness, soups, curries and stews make
satisfying suppers and are packed with
nutritious ingredients, making them
the ultimate feel-good comfort food.
Although you can enjoy these recipes all
year round, nothing beats a warming and
cosy bowl of soup or a spicy curry when
there's a chill in the air.

"Soothing, nurturing and energizing after a long day, these recipes can make you feel like a new person by the time you've wiped the bowl clean."

I have dozens of recipes for belly-warming stews and soups in my archives but these are firmly my favourites – the ones I make over and over again without ever getting tired of them. These recipes span the globe, from my Indonesian-inspired Tempeh Curry, Italian Polpette & Piselli and West African-inspired Peanut Stew, to Moroccan-inspired Lentil & Carrot Soup. Homemade soups and stews offer a big dose of nourishment in every bite, particularly if you use seasonal and locally grown produce. A piping-hot soup is one of my staple weekly meals. It's also one of the most convenient ways to enjoy hot food on the go or at your desk, sipped straight from an insulated flask. I also love a soup as an evening meal, as it's a bit lighter and easier to digest. One of my favourites during winter is my Parsnip, Apple & Leek Soup, which celebrates humble produce, and in spring I love my Asparagus & Pea Soup for a more refreshing meal to celebrate the change of seasons.

Most of the recipes in this chapter only require one pot, making them particularly good for weeknight suppers. Quick to prepare and easy to clean up after, they can be batch cooked and stored ahead of time, ready to warm through for a hearty, perfectly balanced meal. The multitude of ingredients in many of the recipes guarantees you will hit your daily veg targets. Soothing, nurturing and energizing after a long day, these soups can make you feel like a new person by the time you've wiped the bowl clean. The other soup-er thing about a luscious liquid lunch or supper is that they are wonderfully inexpensive.

You can make a simple soup or stew more nutritionally dense by adding an array of toppings such as toasted nuts and seeds, a sprinkle of nutritional yeast for a cheesy hit, some chopped herbs for an injection of freshness, or even broken Rosemary & Fennel Buckwheat Crackers (page 219) used as croutons. Drizzle over some homemade Gremolata (page 129) for a decorative swirl and finish it off with a spoonful of any of my Sprinkles (pages 104–107) for an extra hit of flavour and crunch.

Black Dhal

Since moving to England, I have unashamedly become a bit of a curry monster. I could have literally bathed in the black dhal dish I used to order at a restaurant in London when I first arrived, but as it wasn't plant-based, I tragically had to cut it from my diet. It was a dish that occupied my thoughts, though, so a few years ago I decided that I would try and replicate it, giving it a Happy Skin twist. It might not be exactly like the original recipe I first enjoyed, but I like to think it is certainly on a par with it when it comes to palate pleasure. Lentils, apart from being a wonderful source of iron, protein and fibre, are also rich in vitamin B7, known as biotin. Biotin is right there at the front line of the fight against ageing, with its role in fatty acid synthesis, crucial for healthy skin.

The list of spices here might seem long, but trust me, they will really transform a humble lentil dhal into something spectacular, which you will want to make over and over again! Although this is pretty delicious on its own, I like to serve it with rice, and my Curried Greens (page 236) on the side for a boost of antioxidant-rich vegetables.

SERVES 4

200g dry beluga lentils
2 cloves
1 star anise
2 cardamom pods
1 tbsp fennel seeds
1 tsp ground cumin
1 tsp garam masala
1 tsp smoked paprika
1 tbsp coconut oil, for cooking
1 onion, finely chopped
3 garlic cloves, crushed
1 tbsp freshly grated ginger
½ x 400g tin of chopped tomatoes
1 x 400ml tin of coconut milk
salt, to taste

SERVE WITH:

rice of your choice
chopped fresh coriander
an extra drizzle of coconut milk

Rinse the lentils, then put them into a large pan and cover them with plenty of cold water. Bring to the boil and cook the lentils for 40–50 minutes, until they are soft but still hold their shape. Drain.

Put the cloves, star anise, cardamom pods, fennel seeds, ground cumin, garam masala and smoked paprika into a dry frying pan. Toast the spices on a medium heat for 30–40 seconds, stirring constantly to prevent them burning. Transfer the spices to a spice grinder and blitz until you have a fairly fine powder. If you don't have a spice grinder you can use a pestle and mortar.

Put the coconut oil into a large pan on a medium heat and when it's hot, add the chopped onion. Cook on a medium heat for 5-8 minutes, until it starts to caramelize. Add the garlic and ginger and cook for another couple of minutes, stirring from time to time so it doesn't stick and burn. Add the ground spices and stir to combine. Add the drained lentils, chopped tomatoes, coconut milk and 200ml of water. Mix everything together, then turn the heat down to a simmer and put the lid on. Cook for 45–50 minutes, until the mixture has a thick soupy consistency. Add a bit more water if needed.

Season with salt and serve with rice, chopped fresh coriander and a drizzle of coconut milk.

Chickpea & Almond Curry

A one-pot wonder, this simple curry is ambrosial, perfect for meal prep, budget-friendly, and therefore one of my regular weeknight dinners! The coconut sauce is thick and creamy thanks to the ground almonds and coconut milk, while the ginger and lime juice add a refreshing tangy note. Chickpeas are definitely one of my store-cupboard heroes. They are super-versatile and loaded with skin-boosting antioxidants, protein and fibre. They make this curry really filling, and they also help to regulate your blood sugar levels for stable energy and clearer skin. I can devour this curry simply in a bowl on its own, or make it a bit more special with brown basmati rice and fresh coriander.

SERVES 4

1 tbsp melted coconut oil, for cooking
1 white onion, finely chopped
4 garlic cloves, finely chopped
a thumb-size piece of ginger, grated
1 tsp ground cumin
1 tsp ground coriander
½ tsp ground turmeric
2 tbsp tomato purée
1 x 400ml tin of full-fat coconut milk
3 tbsp ground almonds
1 tbsp smooth almond butter
1 x 400g tin of chickpeas, drained and rinsed
2 generous handfuls of baby spinach
juice of ½ a lime
salt and pepper, to taste

SERVE WITH:
rice of your choice (I have used long-grain brown rice)
chopped fresh coriander

Put the coconut oil into a large pan on a medium heat. When it's hot, add the chopped onion and sauté for 5–8 minutes, until it starts to caramelize. Add the garlic and ginger and cook for another couple of minutes, then add the ground cumin, ground coriander and turmeric. Stir everything together and add the tomato purée. Cook for 1 more minute. Using a hand blender or a small food processor, blitz everything until you have a fairly smooth paste. Add the coconut milk, ground almonds and almond butter, stir everything together and cook on a low simmer for 10 minutes. Add the drained chickpeas and cook for another 10 minutes.

Mix in the baby spinach and cook for another couple of minutes, until it has wilted. Season with salt, pepper and lime juice.

Serve with rice of your choice and a sprinkling of chopped coriander.

Indonesian-style Tempeh Curry

I first had a tempeh curry when I visited Bali and I have been hooked ever since. I have been making my own version at home, and the spice combination is out of this world. The star anise and cinnamon bring in warmth and sweetness, which is perfectly balanced by the tamarind paste and the punch of the lemongrass, ginger and chillies. The tempeh soaks up all the flavours beautifully while adding substantial plant-based protein, iron, calcium and fibre. I love adding green beans, as they are a great source of silicon, which strengthens connective tissues, keeping your skin and nails flexible and strong.

I know there are quite a few ingredients in this curry, but don't be intimated by them. Together they create the most fragrant, creamy dish.

SERVES 2–3

1 white onion, chopped into quarters
3 garlic cloves, chopped
a thumb-size piece of ginger, peeled
1–2 red chillies, chopped
2 sticks of lemongrass, tough outer layers removed, and trimmed
1 tsp ground turmeric
2 tsp ground coriander
1 tsp ground cumin
2 tsp coconut sugar
1 tbsp coconut oil, for cooking
1 tsp tamarind paste
3 star anise
1 stick of cinnamon
1 x 400ml tin of full-fat coconut milk
300g tempeh, cut into chunks
200g green beans, trimmed and cut in half
salt, to taste

SERVE WITH:
brown basmati rice
chopped fresh coriander
sliced red chilli (optional)

Put the onion, garlic, ginger, chillies, lemongrass, turmeric, coriander, cumin and coconut sugar into a food processor and blitz until you have a fairly smooth paste.

Put the coconut oil into a large pan and when it's hot, add the paste from the food processor. Cook on a medium heat for 8–10 minutes, until most of the liquid has evaporated. Add the tamarind paste and stir to combine.

Add the star anise, cinnamon stick and coconut milk. Stir everything and cook for another 10 minutes. Add the tempeh chunks, then turn down to a simmer and cook for another 30 minutes, until you have a rich and thick sauce. Halfway through, add the green beans.

Taste and adjust the seasoning.

Serve with brown basmati rice and chopped coriander, and sliced red chilli if you like.

Polpette & Piselli

This recipe comes straight from my Italian childhood. My mum would always make a batch of polpette (meatballs) at the start of the week and she would serve them in a rich tomato sauce with piselli (peas). This is my nostalgic, plant-based tribute to the recipe. I have used lentils combined with walnuts to recreate that 'meaty' texture, and I inject flavour by adding nutritional yeast, herbs, spices, garlic and onion. The addition of walnuts packs in skin-strengthening omega-3 fatty acids, which help to lower inflammation for clearer and happier skin. I prefer to make my own tomato sauce, which I also use with pasta, but if you are short of time feel free to switch in a shop-bought one.

MAKES 20–23 BALLS, DEPENDING ON THE SIZE

FOR THE POLPETTE:

185g large dried brown/green lentils (not the small beluga or French lentils)
2 tbsp chia seeds, ground in a coffee/spice grinder
4 tbsp olive oil
1 white onion, finely chopped
3 garlic cloves, crushed
2 rosemary sprigs, leaves removed and finely chopped
1 tsp smoked paprika
100g walnuts
2 tbsp nutritional yeast
2 tbsp brown miso paste
110g gluten free or regular breadcrumbs
salt and pepper, to taste

FOR THE PEA AND TOMATO SAUCE:

1 tbsp olive oil
1 white onion, finely chopped
3 garlic cloves, crushed
2 x 400g tins of chopped tomatoes
1 tbsp tomato purée
a bunch of basil (about 20g), chopped + extra for sprinkling on top
200g frozen peas
salt and pepper, to taste

Start by making the polpette. Rinse the lentils and put them into a large pan. Cover with plenty of boiling water and cook for 15–20 minutes, until the lentils are soft but not too mushy. Drain and leave them to cool. In the meantime in a small bowl mix the ground chia seeds with 6 tablespoons of water. Let the mixture sit for at least 10 minutes until you have a gloopy consistency.

Put 1 tablespoon of the olive oil into a large pan on a medium heat and, once hot, add the chopped onion. Cook for 5–8 minutes until it starts to caramelize, then add the crushed garlic, chopped rosemary, smoked paprika and a pinch of salt. Cook for another 2 minutes until the garlic is fragrant. Remove from the heat.

Put the walnuts into a food processor and blitz until they form a fine crumble. Add the cooked lentils, onion mixture, chia mixture, nutritional yeast, miso paste, breadcrumbs and a pinch each of salt and pepper. Pulse a few times until well combined. Don't over-process it, as you want a chunky consistency, not a purée.

Wet your hands (so the mixture won't stick) and roll the lentil dough into golfball-size balls. Put them on a plate and transfer them to the fridge to firm up for 30 minutes.

Put the remaining 3 tablespoons of oil into a large frying pan on a medium-high heat and, once hot, cook the 'meatballs' in batches. Cook them on each side for 3–4 minutes. Toss them around in the pan from time to time so the balls get cooked evenly. You might need to add a bit more oil if the pan becomes too dry.

While the meatballs are cooking, make the pea and tomato sauce. Put the oil and onion into a large pan on a medium heat with a pinch of salt and cook for 5–8 minutes, until it starts to caramelize. Add the crushed garlic and cook for another minute until fragrant. Add

the chopped tomatoes, tomato purée and a dash of water and stir everything to combine. Cook on a medium heat for 10 minutes. Using a hand blender or a regular blender, blend the sauce until smooth. Add the chopped basil and frozen peas and cook for 5 more minutes. Dot the meatballs around and gently shake the pan so they get coated in the tomato sauce. Cook for a final 5 minutes, and serve with some extra basil leaves and a twist of black pepper.

Curried Red Lentil & Butternut Squash Soup

A ravishing autumn supper, this hale and hearty soup is protein-packed and incredibly nourishing. Butternut is my favourite squash, as it has the highest content of vitamin C and vitamin A, both important in countering the damaging effects of free radicals. This soup is creamy, nutritious and brimming with palate-popping nuances thanks to the warm spices. Serve with coconut yogurt for an extra dollop of creaminess, and pumpkin seeds for crunch.

SERVES 4

½ a medium butternut squash, peeled, deseeded and chopped into cubes
2 tbsp melted coconut oil
2 tsp ground turmeric
1 white onion, finely chopped
2 garlic cloves, crushed
1 tbsp curry powder
1 tsp ground cumin
100g split red lentils
500ml veggie stock
1 x 400ml tin of coconut milk
a squeeze of lime juice
salt and pepper, to taste

SERVE WITH:
a dollop of coconut yogurt
a sprinkle of pumpkin seeds
chilli flakes (optional)

Preheat the oven to 220°C/200°C fan/gas 7.

Put the butternut squash cubes on a large baking tray, drizzle with 1 tablespoon of the melted coconut oil and sprinkle over the turmeric and a generous pinch of salt. Toss the butternut squash cubes around so they get evenly coated. Roast in the oven for 25 minutes, until soft.

Meanwhile, put the remaining coconut oil into a large pan on a medium heat. Once hot, add the chopped onions and sauté for 5–8 minutes, until they start to caramelize. Add the garlic, curry powder and cumin and mix everything together, then cook for another minute, stirring continuously to prevent the mixture from burning. Add the lentils, veggie stock and coconut milk and mix everything together. Turn the heat down to a simmer and cook for around 25 minutes, until the lentils are mushy.

Remove the butternut squash from the oven and add it to the lentils, then mix everything well and cook for another couple of minutes. Season with salt and pepper and blend with a hand blender until smooth and creamy. Add a squeeze of lime juice and serve with a dollop of plain coconut yogurt and a sprinkle of pumpkin seeds (and a sprinkle of chilli flakes if you like).

Cauliflower & Pea Curry

Easy, creamy and lightly spiced, this 30-minute cauliflower and pea curry is fantastic fuss-free comfort food. I often make it during the colder months for a cosy dinner when temperatures drop. The unassuming cauliflower is really the star of the skin show here, adding vitamin C and antioxidants, essential for boosting collagen and improving skin texture. This warming coconutty curry is certainly satisfying enough to stand on its own, but a scoop of brown rice and a sprinkle of fresh coriander are welcome additions.

SERVES 3–4

2 tbsp coconut oil, for cooking
1 white onion, finely chopped
1 red chilli, finely chopped
4 garlic cloves, crushed
a thumb-size piece of ginger, grated
5 cardamom pods
1 tsp ground turmeric
1 tsp garam masala
1 tsp ground coriander
½ tsp smoked paprika
340g tomato passata
1 large head of cauliflower, cut into florets
1 x 400ml tin of full-fat coconut milk
1 tsp coconut sugar
120g frozen peas
2 tbsp coconut yogurt
salt and pepper, to taste

SERVE WITH:
chopped fresh coriander
rice of your choice (I have used long-grain brown rice)

Put 1 tablespoon of the coconut oil into a large pan on a medium heat. Once hot, add the onion and cook for 5–8 minutes, until it starts to caramelize. Add the chopped chilli, garlic and ginger and cook for 1 more minute. Bash the cardamom pods in a pestle and mortar – discard the thick husks and add the seeds to the pan together with ½ teaspoon of the turmeric, the garam masala, ground coriander and paprika. Stir everything together and cook for another minute, until the spices are fragrant. Add the passata. Turn down to a simmer and cook for 20–25 minutes.

Meanwhile, preheat the oven to 200°C/180°C fan/gas 6.

Put the cauliflower florets on a large baking tray. Sprinkle with the remaining ½ teaspoon of turmeric, the rest of the coconut oil, some salt and pepper and roast in the oven for 25 minutes, until soft. Once the cauliflower is cooked, remove from the oven.

Using a hand blender, blend the tomato sauce until smooth. Add the coconut milk and coconut sugar, together with the frozen peas. Stir to combine, then mix in the roasted cauliflower and cook for 2–3 minutes.

Add the coconut yogurt and a handful of chopped coriander, stir everything together and serve with rice.

Parsnip, Apple & Leek Soup

Parsnips generally don't get the appreciation that I think they totally deserve. For example, did you know that just half a cup of raw parsnip has 28 per cent of your recommended daily vitamin C intake? And even when cooked, they still provide a good dose of this beautifying vitamin, which is essential for collagen production. They are also rich in an array of other vitamins and minerals like potassium (important for heart health), zinc (great to help prevent breakouts), and vitamins K and E. I absolutely adore them in this radiant and robust soup. The Jazz apple and leek add a hint of sweetness, which is balanced by the earthy, woody notes of the parsnips. Serve with a sprinkle of my Roasted Tamari Super-seed Mix (page 107) for extra crunch and skin-loving minerals and fats.

SERVES 2

1 tbsp olive oil, for cooking
1 leek, sliced
2 garlic cloves, finely chopped
½ tbsp fresh rosemary
1 Jazz apple, core and seeds removed and chopped into pieces
3 medium parsnips, peeled and chopped
½ tbsp white miso paste
700ml veggie stock
salt and pepper, to taste

SERVE WITH:
a sprinkle of my Roasted Tamari Super-seed Mix (page 107)
a drizzle of coconut milk (optional)

Put the oil into a pan on a medium heat. Once hot, add the sliced leek and cook for 8–10 minutes, until the leek has softened and starts to caramelize. Add the garlic and rosemary, stir to combine, then cook for another minute, until the garlic is fragrant. Add the chopped apple, parsnips and miso paste.

Mix everything together and cover with the veggie stock. Turn down the heat to a simmer and cook with the lid on for 20–25 minutes, until the parsnips are soft when pierced with a fork. Check for seasoning, then, using a hand blender or normal blender, blend until smooth and creamy. Serve with a generous sprinkle of Roasted Tamari Super-seed Mix and a drizzle of coconut milk (optional).

Moroccan-inspired Lentil & Carrot Soup

When my fridge is bare, this soup is always a saviour as it requires only a few ingredients. Don't be fooled by the simplicity of this dish, though – it's a taste sensation and it's also nourishing and nutritious, thanks to the tiny but mighty lentil. Lentils are my leading legume when it comes to beauty – they are a great source of folate, an important nutrient for cell repair, and they are packed with protein and fibre, both essential for maintaining stable blood sugar levels. This is important for clear skin because the opposite – fluctuating blood sugar and insulin spikes – can result in breakouts.

Because of lentils' high-fibre content, this soup will keep you feeling full and satiated for longer. Goodbye 4 p.m. slump!

SERVES 4

1 tbsp olive oil, for cooking
1 white onion, finely chopped
1 stick of celery, finely chopped
2 medium carrots, thinly sliced
2 garlic cloves, crushed
½ tsp ground cumin
1 tsp ground coriander
1 tsp smoked paprika
½ tsp ground turmeric
200g dried lentils, rinsed
1 litre veggie stock
a handful of baby spinach
   (optional)
salt and pepper, to taste

SERVE WITH:

a sprinkle of chopped fresh
   coriander
a dollop of plain coconut yogurt

Put the oil into a large pan on a medium heat. Once hot, add the chopped onion, celery and carrots. Cook for 8–10 minutes, until the onion becomes translucent. Add the crushed garlic, cumin, coriander, smoked paprika and turmeric. Stir everything together and cook for another couple of minutes. Make sure you keep stirring, as the garlic can burn really easily.

Add the lentils and veggie stock and stir to combine, then cover with a lid and turn the heat down to a simmer. Cook for 25–30 minutes, until the lentils are soft and the sauce has thickened up. Season to taste and add the baby spinach (if using). Cook for a couple of more minutes, until the spinach has wilted.

Serve with a dollop of coconut yogurt and a sprinkle of coriander.

TIP
This soup freezes really well, so it's a great recipe for meal prepping or batch cooking. If you have any leftovers, store them in the fridge for 3–4 days.

Asparagus & Pea Soup

This is my number-one soup when spring finally arrives. The evenings might still be chilly but as you feel a change in the air during the day, all of a sudden you crave something lighter and fresher.

The star of the show in this soup is the asparagus. The new British season is always something I look forward to, and the tasty little green spears are more powerful than they look. Full of skin-feeding nutrients such as vitamins C and E, they are also rich in glutathione, one of the most powerful antioxidants to help prevent premature ageing. Pair them with the sweetness of the peas, another super-seasonal spring ingredient, which are also loaded with plant protein, vitamins C and E and zinc to really make your skin sing with joy!

SERVES 4

a drizzle of olive oil, for cooking
1 leek, sliced
1 stick of celery, finely chopped
3 garlic cloves, crushed
1 courgette, sliced
800ml veggie stock
300g fresh or frozen peas
½ x 400g tin of cannellini beans, drained and rinsed
200g asparagus, hard ends removed and the rest chopped
100ml tinned coconut milk (optional)
salt and pepper, to taste

SERVE WITH:

a drizzle of good quality extra virgin olive oil
a sprinkle of my Roasted Tamari Super-seed Mix (page 107)

Put a drizzle of olive oil into a large pan on a medium heat. Once hot, add the leek and celery and cook for 10–12 minutes, until the leek has reduced in volume and starts to caramelize. Add the crushed garlic and cook for another 1–2 minutes. Make sure you stir continuously to prevent the garlic from burning.

Add the courgette, plus a little bit of the stock so it doesn't burn, and cook for another 5 minutes. Add the peas, cannellini beans, asparagus and the rest of the veggie stock and cook for a final 5–8 minutes. Using a hand blender or a regular blender, blend the soup until smooth and creamy (you can set some whole peas and asparagus aside before blending if you like, to serve on top of the blended soup). Check for seasoning and add the coconut milk (if using).

Serve with a drizzle of extra virgin olive oil and a sprinkle of my Roasted Tamari Super-seed Mix.

West African-inspired Peanut Stew

Made in one pot, this easy stew is a warm and comforting meal for any season. I absolutely adore the nuttiness of the peanut butter, which goes so well with the sweet potato and the fiery kick from the chillies. Black beans, thanks to their dark skin, are particularly rich in antioxidants and vitamin C. Black beans, like all legumes, are also high in plant-based protein, which helps to regulate blood sugar levels, key for healthy and clear skin. Thick and hearty, this peanut stew is ready in about 30 minutes and is great for leftovers, batch cooking and freezing, making it a perfect midweek lunch or dinner.

SERVES 4

1 tbsp olive oil, for cooking
1 white onion, finely chopped
2 chillies, finely chopped
3 garlic cloves, crushed
2 tbsp grated ginger
1 tbsp ground coriander
2 tsp ground cumin
1 x 400g tin of black beans or
    red kidney beans, drained and
    rinsed
350–400g sweet potatoes, peeled
    and cut into cubes
1 x 400g tin of chopped tomatoes
400ml veggie stock
4 tbsp smooth peanut butter
1 tbsp lemon juice
a handful of baby spinach
    (optional)
salt and pepper, to taste

SERVE WITH:
rice of your choice (I used
    brown basmati rice)
a handful of chopped fresh
    coriander
a sprinkle of toasted peanuts

Put the olive oil into a large pan on a medium heat. Once hot, add the chopped onion and cook for 5–8 minutes, until the onion starts to caramelize. Add the chillies, garlic and ginger and cook for another 1–2 minutes, making sure you stir to prevent burning. Add the coriander and cumin and stir everything to combine.

Add the drained beans, chopped sweet potatoes and chopped tomatoes and stir everything together. Pour in the veggie stock and stir in the peanut butter. Mix everything well and cover with a lid. Turn down the heat to a simmer and cook for 25 minutes, until the sweet potatoes are cooked through.

Season with salt and pepper and add the lemon juice and baby spinach (if using). Stir to combine, and serve with your rice of choice, chopped coriander and a sprinkle of toasted peanuts.

Kimchi Noodle Soup

This is the kind of soup I always reach for whenever I start to feel a bit run down. It always has the healing power to bring me back to life. It offers full-on flavour thanks to the fiery kimchi, which may be important for supporting our immune system, lowering inflammation and therefore keeping our skin happy and clear. I added a good dose of greens to this soup for texture and for more vitamins and antioxidants.

Don't skip the toppings, as they add a vital crunch and, of course, extra nutrients!

SERVES 2

200g buckwheat noodles
2 tbsp toasted sesame seed oil
2 shallots, finely chopped
2 garlic cloves, crushed
a thumb-size piece of ginger, peeled and grated
1 tbsp white miso paste
800ml veggie stock
120g kimchi (check out my Apple Kimchi recipe on page 258)
120g shiitake mushrooms or any other exotic mushrooms, sliced
150g pak choi or tenderstem broccoli
1 tbsp tamari sauce

SERVE WITH:

1 spring onion, finely chopped
a sprinkle of black or white sesame seeds
a sprinkle of chopped fresh coriander

Cook the noodles according to the packet instructions. Drain them and rinse them under cold water to prevent them sticking. Leave them to one side.

Put 1 tablespoon of the toasted sesame seed oil into a large pan on a medium heat. Once hot, add the chopped shallots and cook for 8–10 minutes, until they start to caramelize. Add the garlic and ginger and cook for 2 more minutes, making sure you keep stirring as they can burn very easily. Add the white miso paste, stir to combine and pour in the veggie stock. Add the kimchi, mix everything together, then turn the heat down to a simmer and cook for 10 minutes.

In the meantime, cook the mushrooms. Put the remaining oil into a frying pan on a medium heat and, once hot, add the mushrooms and the pak choi. Cook for about 10 minutes, until the mushrooms start to brown around the edges and the pak choi has softened. I like my pak choi quite al dente, but if you prefer yours a bit softer cook them both for a bit longer. Add the tamari sauce and toss everything together, then remove from the heat.

To serve, put some of the cooked noodles at the bottom of each bowl, then pour over the kimchi broth until the bowl is full. Add your pan-fried mushrooms and pak choi. Finish it off with the chopped spring onion, sesame seeds and coriander.

TIP
You can make the broth in advance and store it in the fridge for a few days. Just cook your noodles and vegetables when it comes to serving. You can use rice noodles if you prefer.

Creamy Cannellini, Mushroom & Cavolo Nero Stew

Whenever I head back to the countryside around Bologna where I grew up, this is the first dish I will always cook. My dad, whose diet consists of about 95 per cent beans and cabbage, has a garden overflowing with emerald-green cavolo nero (also called Tuscan kale) plants. As with most Italian dishes, this recipe is about quality ingredients, cooked simply to allow them to sing. The cannellini beans, when blended, help create a luxurious creamy, thick stew without the need for any cream. It's no secret that kale is good for you, but did you know that just 50g of raw kale delivers over 200 per cent of your daily vitamin A (a powerful vitamin for preventing ageing) and 120 per cent of your daily vitamin C (essential for collagen production)? Pair that with the selenium content of the mushrooms and you have got yourself a wonderfully beautifying winter warmer.

SERVES 4

2 x 400g tins of cannellini beans, drained and rinsed
400ml veggie stock
200ml unsweetened oat milk
2 tbsp olive oil
2 shallots, finely chopped
1 carrot, finely chopped
1 stick of celery, finely chopped
2 garlic cloves, crushed
1 bay leaf
a few sprigs of fresh thyme, leaves picked
½ tbsp white miso paste
½ tbsp tamari sauce + extra for drizzling
50g cavolo nero or kale, de-stemmed and finely chopped
200g mixed mushrooms (I used a mix of chestnut and shiitake), sliced
salt and pepper, to taste

SERVE WITH:

a sprinkle of chopped fresh parsley
a drizzle of good quality extra virgin olive oil

To make the creamy broth, put 120g of cannellini beans into a blender with the veggie stock and oat milk. Blend until smooth, then set to one side.

Put 1 tablespoon of the olive oil into a large pan on a medium heat. When it's hot, add the chopped shallots, carrot and celery. Cook for 8–10 minutes, until the shallots start to caramelize. Add the crushed garlic, bay leaf and thyme leaves and cook for another couple of minutes. Keep stirring, as garlic can burn very easily. Add the miso paste and tamari sauce, stir to combine, then add the remaining cannellini beans and the creamy broth. Turn the heat down to a simmer and cook the stew for 20 minutes, until it has started to thicken. Add the chopped cavolo nero, mix everything together and cook for another 5 minutes, until the cavolo nero has softened.

While the bean stew is simmering away, cook the mushrooms. Put the remaining oil into a frying pan and once it is hot, add the sliced mushrooms. Cook them on a medium heat for 10 minutes, until they start to brown around the edges and all the water has evaporated. Drizzle with tamari sauce and remove from the heat.

Serve the cannellini stew with the pan-fried mushrooms piled on top, a sprinkle of chopped parsley and a drizzle of extra virgin olive oil.

Bountiful Salads

If you are not the biggest fan of salads, I get you – I wasn't either. Until I transformed my diet, I always ate the wrong kind of salad: those boring iceberg lettuce, cucumber and tomato ones (maybe with a little sweetcorn if I was lucky). They certainly weren't tasty or particularly nutritious. There's nothing bog-standard about the recipes in this chapter, however. They've all been thoughtfully created to wow your taste buds and make you feel full.

"Salads are a great way to get in an optimal daily intake of vegetables with just one meal."

My relationship with salads changed as I moved over to plant-based. I knew salads could be a great vessel to pack in a cargo of skin-loving minerals, antioxidants and vitamins. Vitamin C in particular is one of my favourite beauty vitamins, as it supports collagen production which is what makes your skin bouncy and plump. Vitamin C unfortunately is heat-sensitive, meaning that some is lost during the cooking process. Salads are also a wonderful way to get in an optimal daily intake of vegetables with just one meal, and are excellent for ensuring plenty of plant diversity in your diet, which is essential for gut health.

When I embarked on my healthy culinary odyssey, I quickly discovered that one of the key elements to a great salad is a proper dressing. A delicious dressing is the easiest way to inject any salad with lots of zest, zing and flavour. Sadly, shop-bought dressings are usually full of sugar and unhealthy fats, which is why I always prefer to make my own. It only takes 5 minutes, and you can make them in advance and store them in the fridge for a few days. Every salad recipe in this chapter has a mouth-watering dressing, and you will also find my 4 most-used everyday dressings at the end of the chapter.

As well as a dressing packed with flavour, a scrumptious salad needs texture and contrast. Some of my favourites when I crave something hearty are my Cauliflower & Puy Lentil Salad, with the creamiest roasted garlic and coconut yogurt dressing, and my Rainbow Noodle Salad, with a tangy peanut butter dressing. If I crave something a bit lighter, my Spring Picnic Salad with avocado mayo dressing or my Sunshine Slaw with a nutty almond butter dressing are always winners.

Cauliflower & Puy Lentil Salad

This warm cauliflower and lentil salad is the perfect midweek dinner. Less than 30 minutes, one pan and lots of deliciousness. Although the average cauliflower might not have the most vibrant colour, this humble veg definitely brings lots of nutrition to the table and to your skin! One of the most important compounds in cauliflower is sulforaphane, which may have anti-cancer properties and supports heart health in various ways. The anti-inflammatory compounds of this vegetable help in preventing skin conditions such as acne, rosacea and eczema.

The curried coconut yogurt marinade is so moreish, and turns the humble cauliflower into something extra scrumptious. To make this salad even more delectable and filled with goodness, I've added scarlet-red pomegranate seeds and crunchy flaked almonds. The pomegranate seeds not only add a note of tart sweetness to the dish but bring an incredible array of antioxidants to the party, which as we know are important in helping to prevent premature ageing.

SERVES 2

1 head of cauliflower
80g unsweetened coconut yogurt
2 tbsp olive oil
1 tbsp curry powder
½ tbsp ground coriander
250g cooked Puy lentils
a generous handful of toasted
    flaked almonds
seeds of ½ a pomegranate
salt and pepper, to taste

FOR THE DRESSING:

100g unsweetened coconut yogurt
juice of ½ a lemon
1 tbsp olive oil
1 garlic clove, crushed
a handful of fresh mint, finely
    chopped + extra to serve
a handful of fresh coriander
    leaves, finely chopped + extra
    to serve
a generous sprinkle of salt and
    pepper

Preheat the oven to 220°C/200°C fan/gas 7 and line a large baking tray with parchment paper.

Divide the cauliflower into florets, keeping the leaves and chopping them into bite-size pieces. Put the coconut yogurt, olive oil, curry powder and ground coriander into a large bowl and mix it all together. Add the cauliflower florets and leaves and toss everything so the cauliflower is evenly coated in the marinade. I find it works best to do this with my hands.

Season with salt and pepper. Spread the cauliflower on the lined baking tray and roast in the oven for 20 minutes. Change the oven to the grill setting and place the cauliflower tray right under the heat. Grill for 5–8 minutes, until the cauliflower is slightly charred around the edges.

While the cauliflower is cooking, make the dressing. Simply put all the ingredients into a bowl and mix until well combined. Season with salt and pepper.

Serve the roasted cauliflower while still hot, with the Puy lentils, flaked almonds, pomegranate seeds and the coconut dressing. Finish with a sprinkle of coriander and mint leaves.

TIP
Although this salad is best enjoyed warm, it also makes a delicious lunchbox the next day. Just keep the dressing separate and stir through when you are ready to eat.

Rainbow Noodle Salad

We now know that eating a wide variety of plant-based foods is very important for supporting our gut health, which heavily influences pretty much every function of our body, including our skin. This is a ravishing salad, packing in lots of vibrant and colourful vegetables, all tied together by a punchy peanut dressing. The raw peppers are bursting with collagen-boosting vitamin C, the carrots are a powerhouse of anti-ageing vitamin A, and the purple cabbage is popping with antioxidants for defending our skin against free radicals. I love this salad – it comes together in no time, it's packed with flavour and it's very filling, thanks to the complex carbohydrates from the buckwheat noodles. It also makes a great lunchbox – just pop the dressing into a separate container and drizzle it on the salad just before serving.

SERVES 2

200g buckwheat noodles
a drizzle of toasted sesame seed oil
2 carrots, cut into really thin
    matchsticks
1 red, green or yellow pepper,
    deseeded and cut into thin
    matchsticks
60g purple cabbage, shredded
3 spring onions, finely sliced
½ a cucumber, cut into thin
    matchsticks
150g cooked edamame beans

FOR THE DRESSING:
3 tbsp runny and smooth peanut
    butter
1 tbsp tamari sauce
1 tbsp toasted sesame seed oil
juice of ½ a lime
½ tbsp maple syrup
½ tbsp finely grated ginger
2 garlic cloves, crushed

SERVE WITH:
a handful of chopped fresh
    coriander
a sprinkle of lightly toasted white
    sesame seeds

Cook the buckwheat noodles according to the packet instructions. Drain, then rinse them under cold water to stop the cooking process. Transfer them to a bowl and lightly drizzle them with the toasted sesame seed oil to prevent them sticking together.

To make the dressing, simply put all the ingredients into a bowl and mix until smooth. Add 2 tablespoons of cold water to thin it out, then mix again.

Add all the vegetables and edamame beans to the bowl of noodles. Pour over the peanut butter dressing and mix everything together. Serve with a generous sprinkle of chopped coriander and toasted sesame seeds.

Balsamic Beetroot with Whipped Tahini Cream

I must admit I wasn't the biggest fan of beetroots until I learnt about all their incredible skin benefits. They definitely have a slight 'muddy' flavour that often puts people off, but this was the game-changer recipe that made me fall in love with them. The balsamic vinegar adds a gentle sweetness and at the same time a smack of sharpness, which transforms the humble beets into something extra-special.

Beetroots contain collagen-building vitamins, iron, beta-carotene and lycopene. The whipped tahini cream is other-worldly good and a total revelation. Fluffy, creamy and rich, it provides a beautiful base for the earthy roast beets as well as containing beautifying minerals like zinc and calcium. I added some radicchio leaves not only to make this salad stunning on the plate but also to inject a subtle bitterness, which really balances everything brilliantly. This is the kind of salad that I make when I want to impress family and friends, because it just looks so beautiful, but it's also perfect as a light meal.

SERVES 2

370–400g raw beetroots
2 tbsp balsamic vinegar
1 tbsp olive oil
40g hazelnuts
50–70g radicchio or chicory leaves
salt and pepper, to taste

FOR THE WHIPPED TAHINI:

100g runny tahini
juice of ½ a lemon
1 garlic clove, crushed
½ tbsp maple syrup
a pinch of salt

SERVE WITH:

a drizzle of good quality extra
   virgin olive oil
a sprinkle of fresh dill and mint
   leaves

Preheat the oven to 220°C/200°C fan/gas 7.

Trim and peel the beetroots. Cut them into quarters and put them on a large baking tray with the balsamic vinegar, olive oil, and season with salt and pepper. Gently toss until the beets are evenly coated. Cover the tray with kitchen foil and roast in the oven for 30 minutes, then remove the foil and roast uncovered for another 25 minutes, until the beets are tender.

Put the hazelnuts on a small baking tray and toast them in the oven for the last 5 minutes.

To make the whipped tahini, put the tahini, lemon juice, crushed garlic, maple syrup and salt into a food processor. Pulse for just a few seconds, until the ingredients are combined, adding 100ml cold water through the feed tube. Scrape the sides a few times, then pulse again until the mixture has a pillowy and creamy consistency.

Spread the whipped tahini in a circle on a serving plate. Top with the roasted beetroots and scatter over the toasted hazelnuts and roughly chopped radicchio. Serve with a generous drizzle of extra virgin olive oil and a few dill and mint leaves.

Warm Sweet Potato Noodle Salad

I treasure this salad because it is such an interesting way to jazz up sweet potatoes and turn them into nourishing noodles. As you probably know by now, sweet potatoes are one of my top beauty foods. Did you know that just one baked sweet potato will help you far surpass your recommended daily dose of vitamin A? They are also a wonderful source of vitamins C and B6. All these vitamins work in harmony to boost collagen and speed up cell turnover for glowing and supple skin.

Tossed with red pepper, broccoli and edamame beans and coated in a creamy tahini sauce, this unique and scrumptious salad comes together in under 30 minutes.

SERVES 2

2 sweet potatoes
1 tbsp toasted sesame seed oil
1 red, green or yellow pepper,
    deseeded and thinly sliced
½ a head of broccoli, chopped into
    small florets
150g frozen edamame beans

FOR THE SAUCE:
3 tbsp runny tahini
1 tbsp brown miso paste
1 tsp maple syrup
juice of ½ a lime
2 garlic cloves, crushed
1 tbsp grated ginger

SERVE WITH:
2 spring onions, sliced
a handful of chopped fresh
    coriander
a sprinkle of black sesame seeds

To make the sauce, simply put all the ingredients into a bowl together with 4 tablespoons of cold water and mix well, until creamy and smooth. Set aside.

Peel and spiralize the sweet potatoes, using either a spiralizer or a vegetable peeler. Put the oil into a large frying pan on a medium heat. Throw in the sweet potato noodles, cover with a lid and cook for around 8 minutes, until they start to soften. Remove from the pan and transfer them to a plate. Set aside.

Add the pepper and broccoli to the pan. Add an extra drizzle of oil if needed. Cook for 10 minutes, then put back the sweet potato noodles and add the frozen edamame beans. Stir everything together and cook for another 5–8 minutes, until the sweet potato noodles are fully cooked. They should be soft but still have a bite.

Pour over the sauce, mix well, and serve while still hot, with the chopped spring onions, coriander and sesame seeds scattered over.

Roasted White Cabbage with Lentil Chimichurri

I first had this dish when I went to the restaurant Plants by DE in London and remember thinking, 'How can a cabbage taste so good!' Following the visit, I started to make my own version at home and even my carnivore boyfriend would polish off every last bit. It's so tasty, it had to make it into this book.

Undoubtedly white cabbage isn't the most appetizing or Hollywood of vegetables, but when you roast it in the oven it turns into something spectacular and Oscar-worthy. It maintains a crunchy bite, but it becomes slightly sweeter than its raw version. Although white cabbage is often overlooked, it presents an impressive nutritional profile. It's high in vitamin C, which you know by now is essential in boosting collagen production, which helps keep your skin looking plump and supple. The lentil chimichurri adds a feisty freshness and tangy tangent to the dish, while also providing protein and fibre. Parsley in particular is surprisingly rich in vitamin A, which is one of my favourite beauty vitamins, as it helps with cell turnover to keep our skin youthful. The silky tahini dressing is what really unites all these ingredients together in greatness by adding a delicious creaminess to the cabbage and lentils. I know you are going to love it as much as I do!

SERVES 4 AS A SIDE

1 head of white cabbage
1 tsp smoked paprika
2 tbsp olive oil
salt and pepper, to taste
chilli flakes, to serve (optional)

FOR THE LENTIL CHIMICHURRI:

50g green lentils, rinsed
1 shallot, finely chopped
30g parsley, finely chopped
1 tbsp capers, roughly chopped
3 tbsp extra virgin olive oil
1 tbsp red wine vinegar
1 tbsp lemon juice
salt and pepper, to taste

FOR THE TAHINI DRESSING:

4 tbsp runny tahini
1 tsp maple syrup
1 tbsp lemon juice
1 tsp Dijon mustard
salt and pepper, to taste

Cut the white cabbage into quarters and remove the sturdy bit at the bottom. Place the cabbage quarters on a large baking tray. Sprinkle with the smoked paprika, season with salt and pepper, and drizzle with the olive oil. Massage the seasoning into the cabbage slices so they are evenly coated. Roast them in the oven at 200°C/180°C fan/gas 6 for 1 hour.

In the meantime, cook the lentils in plenty of boiling water until they are soft (about 20 minutes). Drain them and allow to cool.

In a large bowl, mix together the shallot, parsley, capers, extra virgin olive oil, vinegar, lemon juice and a generous pinch each of salt and pepper. Add the cooked lentils and mix well. Leave to one side.

To make the tahini dressing, simply mix all the ingredients together in a small bowl and season with salt and pepper. Add 2–3 tablespoons of cold water to thin it out until you have a runny and creamy consistency.

Remove the cabbage from the oven and serve while still warm, with the lentil chimichurri on top and a generous drizzle of the tahini dressing. For an extra spicy kick, add a sprinkle of chilli flakes.

Kale, Apple & Fennel Salad with Avocado Dressing

Saying I used to dislike kale is an understatement. I used to dislike it with a passion. Then I started reading about all its incredible health and skin benefits and I knew I had to give it a proper go. A raw kale salad was probably my idea of hell on a plate, but then I learned the trick of massaging it to make it much softer and more palatable. That was a crucial moment that led me to discover the benefits of pairing kale's natural bitterness with much sweeter and softer fruit or vegetables. For this recipe, I have chosen sweet potato and apple, which work in perfect harmony with the more earthy notes of the kale. I particularly love sweet potatoes, as they are a wonderful source of complex carbs (your body will take longer to digest them, keeping you feeling fuller for longer), plus they provide you with a good dose of vitamins A, C and E, all very important antioxidants to keep your skin firm and glowing. The super-creamy avocado and cashew dressing is what really elevates this salad, by adding lots of skin-loving healthy fats and zinc, which can be so helpful in preventing breakouts.

To add a crunchy bite, I sprinkle some maple pecans on top, which adds extra sweetness and a decadent buttery texture.

SERVES 2

1 medium sweet potato, peeled and cut into cubes
a drizzle of olive oil, for roasting
100g curly kale, stems removed, leaves finely chopped
1 apple, core removed, cut into thin slices
1 fennel bulb, trimmed and shaved into thin slices (ideally using a mandoline)
salt and pepper, to taste

FOR THE CANDIED PECANS:

40g pecans, roughly chopped
½ tbsp maple syrup
a pinch of sea salt

FOR THE DRESSING:

50g raw cashews, soaked in boiling water for 30 minutes
1 ripe avocado, peeled, stoned and roughly chopped
juice of 1 lemon
1 garlic clove
3 tbsp extra virgin olive oil
salt and pepper, to taste

Preheat the oven to 220°C/200°C fan/gas 7.

Put the pecans into a dry pan and toast them on a medium heat for 3–4 minutes. Add the maple syrup and a pinch of salt and stir everything together. Remove from the heat and let them cool down completely.

Put the sweet potato cubes on a large baking tray and drizzle with olive oil. Sprinkle with salt and pepper, then toss everything together. Roast in the oven for 25–30 minutes, until soft and crispy around the edges.

While the sweet potato is cooking, make the dressing. Drain the cashews and put them into a blender with all the other dressing ingredients. Blend until smooth and creamy, then set to one side.

Put the chopped kale into a large bowl and pour over the dressing. Using your hands, massage the kale for 2–3 minutes, until the leaves feel softer. Add the apple and fennel to the bowl and mix everything together. Serve with the roasted sweet potato and candied pecans on top.

Spring Picnic Salad

This is by far one of my favourite things to pack if, you guessed it, I am going on a picnic or heading to any kind of al fresco gathering. I particularly love to make this salad in spring, when asparagus is in season, but if I can't get my hands on it, I will use green beans instead. Potatoes tend to get quite a bad rep in the 'wellness' world, and I think it's because we usually fry them or slather them in unhealthy fats or oils, but actually the humble spud certainly chips in when it comes to beauty vitamins and minerals. For example, from one medium potato you get about a third of your anti-ageing vitamin C for the day, as well as potassium and vitamin B6 and other minerals such as iron, manganese, copper, magnesium and phosphorus.

The avocado mayo dressing is what takes this salad to the next level. It's smooth, tangy and rich, and also works well as a dip with roasted vegetables, or when slathered on sandwiches or burritos.

SERVES 2

500g baby or new potatoes, whole
150g asparagus spears, trimmed
    and cut in half
120g fresh or frozen peas
100g radishes, thinly sliced
2 spring onions, finely chopped
a small bunch of fresh mint leaves
    (about 10g), finely chopped
a small bunch of fresh dill (about
    10g), finely chopped

FOR THE AVOCADO MAYO
DRESSING:

1 ripe avocado, peeled, stoned
    and roughly chopped
2 tbsp runny tahini
1 tbsp extra virgin olive oil + extra
    for drizzling
juice of 1 lemon
1 tbsp small capers + 1 tbsp of
    their brine
a generous pinch each of salt
    and pepper

Put the potatoes into a large pan, cover them with boiling water and add a pinch of salt. Cook on a medium heat for 20–25 minutes, until they are soft when pierced with a fork. While your potatoes are cooking, make the dressing. Put all the ingredients into a blender with 1 tablespoon of cold water and blend until smooth.

Once the potatoes are cooked, remove them from the boiling water with a slotted spoon and set them aside to cool down. Save the water. Add the asparagus and peas to the potato water and cook them for 5 minutes. Drain, then put them into a large bowl filled with ice cubes and cold water to stop the cooking process.

Cut the potatoes in half or quarters. If you have any which are very small you can leave them whole. To assemble the salad, put the potatoes, asparagus and peas into a large bowl or on a serving dish and drizzle with a little extra virgin olive oil. Scatter the radishes, spring onions, mint leaves and dill over the top, and serve with the avocado mayo dressing stirred through or dolloped on top.

Sunshine Slaw

The tart, zesty crunch of this cabbage slaw is addictive and it's no longer just a bit on the side – it's the star of the show and fab when we have friends around for a barbecue. I love sweetcorn in the summer months, it pops in the mouth with natural sweetness, making it a textbook addition to any salad. It's also rich in gut-loving fibre, which, paired with all the vitamins and minerals of the other ingredients, means this slaw is an all-season, beautifying side dish.

The key to making this slaw utterly delicious is to make sure all the veg is thinly sliced. For best results, I would recommend using a mandoline for the cabbage, a vegetable peeler for the carrot and a sharp knife for all the other vegetables.

SERVES 4 AS A SIDE

2 sweetcorn cobs
olive oil, for cooking
150g white cabbage, finely
  shredded, ideally with a
  mandoline
1 small romaine lettuce, finely
  sliced
½ a red pepper, thinly sliced
2 medium carrots, peeled into
  julienne or ribbons
3 spring onions, finely chopped
1 red chilli, finely sliced (optional)
a small bunch of fresh mint leaves
  (about 15g), finely chopped
a small bunch of fresh coriander
  (about 15g), finely chopped
a generous sprinkle of my
  Roasted Tamari Super-seed
  Mix (page 107)

FOR THE DRESSING:

3 tbsp runny almond butter
2 tbsp lime juice
1 garlic clove, crushed
½ tbsp grated ginger
1 tbsp toasted sesame seed oil
1 tsp maple syrup
1 tsp white miso paste

Steam or boil the sweetcorn cobs for 8–10 minutes, until the kernels are soft, then drain. Put a drizzle of olive oil into a large griddle pan on a medium heat (you can also do this on your barbecue). Once hot, add the sweetcorn and griddle them on each side for 2–3 minutes, until slightly charred. Remove from the heat and leave them to one side to cool down.

To make the dressing, simply put all the ingredients into a bowl and whisk together until smooth. Add 4 tablespoons of cold water and mix again to achieve a pourable consistency.

Using a short knife, slice off the kernels from the sweetcorn cobs and put them into a large bowl. Add all the sliced vegetables, then pour over the dressing and mix well. Serve with the chopped herbs and the Roasted Tamari Super-seed Mix sprinkled on top.

Red Pesto Traybake Veg Salad

This is one of my favourite speedy dinners, especially during the summer months. It's jam-packed with robust flavours, vegetables and texture, and the red pepper pesto might just be my number-one type of pesto. It's fresh, tangy, creamy and incredibly versatile. You can also use it as a pasta sauce, as a dip or in sandwiches. This salad is also not lacking in skin-nourishing minerals, vitamins and antioxidants, thanks to the wide array of vibrant vegetables. It's filling and satiating, thanks to the high-fibre content and the chickpeas, which also bring a good dose of zinc, a wonderful mineral to help keep those breakouts at bay. It's also a great lunchbox-friendly salad: just stir the pesto through the vegetables but keep the rocket on the side so it stays crispy and fresh.

SERVES 2

1 courgette, sliced
1 small aubergine, cut into small cubes
1 red onion, cut into wedges
½ tsp smoked paprika
½ tbsp dried oregano
a drizzle of olive oil
1 x 400g tin of chickpeas, drained and rinsed
150g cherry tomatoes, whole
60g pitted olives, sliced
2 tbsp small capers
10g fresh basil, roughly chopped
10g fresh parsley, roughly chopped
salt and pepper, to taste
40g rocket, to serve

FOR THE RED PESTO:

1 large pointed red pepper (about 170g), whole
2 tbsp extra virgin olive oil + extra for brushing
40g walnuts
1 garlic clove
1 tbsp lemon juice
1 tbsp nutritional yeast
3 sun-dried tomatoes

Preheat the oven to 220°C/200°C fan/gas 7.

Put the courgette, aubergine and red onion on a large baking tray. Make sure there is plenty of space, as you will need to add the chickpeas and tomatoes later. Sprinkle over the smoked paprika, dried oregano and a pinch each of salt and pepper, and drizzle everything generously with olive oil. Put the pointed red pepper on a separate tray. Brush it with olive oil, and sprinkle with salt and pepper.

Put both trays into the oven. Roast the pointed pepper for 25 minutes, until soft and squishy. Roast the veggies for 15 minutes, then remove from the oven and add the drained chickpeas and cherry tomatoes to the tray. Toss them around so they get evenly coated, and add a little bit more olive oil and salt if needed. Put the tray back into the oven for the final 10 minutes.

To make the pesto, remove the stalk, seeds and skin from the roasted pepper. Put the flesh into a food processor with the rest of the pesto ingredients and blitz everything together until smooth and creamy.

Add the olives, capers, basil and parsley to the tray of roasted veg. Gently mix everything together.

To assemble your salad, arrange the rocket on a large serving dish, then add the roasted veg and chickpea mix. Drizzle over the pesto and mix everything together before serving.

Chilli Broccoli Salad

Broccoli was definitely one of those vegetables I never really liked as a kid. When I started to cook properly, I would always use it, as I knew it was good for me, but I never truly enjoyed it until I started cooking and dressing it correctly. I swapped steaming and boiling for roasting, and that was definitely the game-changer! I also started to get creative with dressings and sauces, like this zesty, tangy and herby dressing, which is what really transforms the humble broccoli into something utterly scrumptious! Broccoli is not only very affordable and widely available but it's also full of many of the vitamins and minerals that are important for skin health, including zinc, vitamin A and vitamin C. It also contains lutein, a carotenoid that works like beta-carotene. Lutein helps protect your skin from oxidative damage, which can cause your skin to become dry and age quicker.

To add some extra skin-loving fats, I have used toasted almonds, which give a delicious crunch and nuttiness to the dish.

SERVES 2

100g black or wild rice
1 head of broccoli, chopped into
    florets
1 red onion, cut into quarters
1 x 400g tin of chickpeas, drained
    and rinsed
olive oil, for roasting
15g almonds, roughly chopped
a small handful of fresh mint
    (about 5g), roughly chopped
a small handful of fresh coriander
    (about 5g), roughly chopped
seeds of ½ a pomegranate
salt and pepper, to taste

FOR THE DRESSING:
5 tbsp extra virgin olive oil
1 tbsp grated ginger
a small handful of fresh coriander
a small handful of fresh mint
juice of 1 lime
3 tsp maple syrup
1 tsp apple cider vinegar
1 green chilli

Preheat the oven to 200°C/180°C fan/gas 6.

Cook the rice according to the packet instructions. Usually, when it comes to black or wild rice, I would recommend soaking it for few hours beforehand to speed up the cooking process.

In the meantime, put the broccoli, red onion and chickpeas on a large baking tray. Drizzle generously with olive oil and sprinkle with salt and pepper. Toss everything and roast in the oven for 25 minutes, until the broccoli is tender.

While the broccoli is roasting, make the dressing. Simply put everything into a blender and blend until smooth.

Put the almonds into a dry pan and toast them on a medium heat for 5 minutes.

Remove the broccoli from the oven and add the cooked rice to the tray. Sprinkle over the chopped herbs, pomegranate seeds and toasted almonds, and serve with the dressing drizzled on top.

Four Life-changing Dressings

My biggest tip for anyone looking to eat more vegetables (and enjoy them!) is to start making healthy salad dressings at home. They are always more flavourful than bottled dressings and they can liven up even the simplest salad. Unlike shop-bought dressings, a homemade dressing isn't designed to keep for months on end. That means it can be made with fresh and vibrant ingredients like herbs, garlic and avocado, which still retain their nutritional profile. They might not last for weeks, but they are brimming with those special skin-loving antioxidants, minerals and vitamins.

These four dressings are fresh, packed with goodness and easy to make. Try them and I promise your salads will never taste so good!

RASPBERRY VINAIGRETTE

This is my favourite vinaigrette to make when the weather warms up and fresh raspberries are in abundance. I absolutely adore its bright pink colour and it also brings a hit of skin-nurturing antioxidants and vitamin C. It's fresh, bright, fruity, sweet and delicious drizzled over a wide range of salad recipes. It goes particularly well with bitter leaves (like rocket, chicory, radicchio etc…) as the raspberries add an injection of natural sweetness.

SERVES 2

100g fresh raspberries
4 tbsp extra virgin olive oil
1 shallot, peeled and roughly chopped
1 tbsp apple cider vinegar
1 tsp Dijon mustard
salt and pepper, to taste

Put all the ingredients in a blender and blend until smooth. Store in an airtight container or jar in the fridge for 2–3 days.

AVOCADO GREEN GODDESS DRESSING

If you love avocado as much as I do, you are going to adore this dressing. It's creamy, smooth and packed with zingy, fresh flavours. It's also a great way to use up overripe avocados (even if they have a few brown spots!) and turn them into a pourable dressing that makes an appetizing addition to any salad.

SERVES 2

1 ripe avocado, peeled, stoned and roughly chopped
2 tbsp lemon juice
2 tbsp extra virgin olive oil
1 garlic clove
the green part of 1 spring onion
10g fresh basil
10g fresh coriander

Simply put everything into a blender with 4 tablespoons of cold water and blend until smooth and creamy. Store in an airtight container or jar in the fridge for 2–3 days.

CASHEW & MISO DRESSING

Cashews are one of my hero ingredients for using in healthy dressings and sauces, as they create a super-creamy consistency without the addition of any cream or mayonnaise. They are very versatile too, and here I particularly love the nutty flavour combined with the saltiness of the miso paste. This dressing is perfect for pretty much any vegetables, but it goes particularly well with raw kale and helps to soften its sturdy leaves.

SERVES 2

80g raw cashews, soaked in boiling water
    for 30 minutes
4 tbsp extra virgin olive oil
2 tbsp white miso paste
2 tbsp apple cider vinegar
2 tbsp lemon juice
2 garlic cloves
2 tsp maple syrup

Drain and rinse the cashews. Put everything into a blender together with 6 tablespoons of cold water and blend until smooth and creamy. Store in an airtight container or jar in the fridge for 2–3 days.

EVERYDAY VINAIGRETTE

This is my much-loved, tried and tested basic vinaigrette, which I have been making for years. It's one of those great dressing recipes to have in your arsenal, as it's so versatile. It's great for any kind of green salad, but also works wonderfully well with roasted vegetables and grain bowls.

SERVES 2

8 tbsp extra virgin olive oil
2 tbsp lemon juice
2 tbsp apple cider vinegar
2 tsp wholegrain mustard
2 tsp maple syrup
2 garlic cloves, crushed
salt and pepper, to taste

Put all the ingredients into a small bowl or jar and mix until well combined. Store in an airtight container or jar in the fridge for 2–3 days.

Beautifying Smoothies & Tonics

When I was trying to find my way to a more a wholesome way of eating to support my skin, one of the first purchases I made was my trusty blender. Back then, I was spending a large part of my days in an office or travelling to work, often doing long hours with very little time to cook. Smoothies quickly became an easy and delicious way to make sure I packed in a hefty amount of fruit and vegetables, which I knew my skin would thank me for. I still often make smoothies for breakfast, sometimes as an alternative to a mid-afternoon snack and often after a workout. In this chapter, you will find four of my favourite smoothies, which I've been drinking non-stop while I've been writing this book!

"What you drink is as important as what you eat."

─────────

They are a bit unusual, as I didn't want to give you a recipe for something you have probably already seen a million times. My Chickpea Chocolate Smoothie is a thick and creamy decadent treat with a natural protein boost, for example. Or there's my Green Pea Smoothie, with lots of skin-loving green peas and avocado – I love this for a speedy breakfast, to keep my energy levels stable throughout the day. They are all utterly delicious and packed with minerals, antioxidants and plant protein to really make you feel nourished from inside out.

What you drink is as important as what you eat. We tend to focus a lot on what we eat but often overlook the importance of hydration. Staying hydrated is absolutely essential for optimal health, and to keep your skin plumped and prevent dryness. Drinking water is of course the best way to stay hydrated, and I usually aim to drink 3 litres of water per day. Adding slices of citrus or cucumber, or some mint leaves, instantly gives it a little bit of flavour (and extra antioxidants!), making it easier to drink if you feel like it's a chore.

In the past few years, I have mastered making a few beautifying drinks and tonics which offer not only hydration but also antioxidants, minerals and vitamins to quench and feed your skin with every sip. Some recipes are warming and calming, perfect for the colder months, like a giant hug in a mug. I love drinking my

Soothing Turmeric Tonic when I am feeling tired or a bit run down. And I love my Wake-me-up Cacao Elixir when I need extra motivation to get out of bed in the morning. They are all wonderfully cosy and I encourage you to use enjoying them as moments of mindfulness and self-care.

In this chapter you will also find refreshing drinks perfect for the summer months, when your skin needs hydration to cope with the heat. I often make my Raspberry & Mint Chia Fresca if I am going on a hike or a long walk, and I love my Hydrating Strawberry & Coconut Lemonade after a sweaty workout.

Chickpea Chocolate Smoothie

Being a huge chocolate-lover, this is probably my all-time favourite smoothie. It's so good, it almost tastes like a dessert. The chickpeas add some filling plant-based protein, fibre and manganese, an important beauty mineral which is known to fight free radicals that can cause wrinkles. They also make the smoothie extra thick and creamy, but I promise, you won't taste them! This healthy chocolate banana smoothie recipe is made with just six ingredients, and is easy to customize with nut butter and extra inclusions like ground cinnamon or vanilla extract. An awe-some breakfast, snack or even dessert!

SERVES 1

2 frozen bananas
2 Medjool dates, pitted
50g cooked chickpeas
1 tbsp nut butter of your choice
   (I have used almond)
2 tbsp raw cacao or cocoa powder
250ml almond milk

Simply put all the ingredients into a blender and blend until smooth and creamy. Add some more almond milk if you would like the smoothie to have a runnier consistency.

Green Pea Smoothie

This smoothie makes a brilliant breakfast or post-workout snack as it gives an incredible protein boost, especially from the peas, hemp seed and almond butter. It might seem a bit strange to add peas to a smoothie, but you will barely know they are there, I promise! Not only are they rich in protein and fibre, peas are also brimming with collagen-boosting vitamin C and folate, which is essential for cell repair. This green smoothie is a simple, healthy and nutrient-dense recipe that will fuel you through your day. Trust me, this is one drink you're going to want to make again and again.

SERVES 1

50g frozen peas
2 frozen bananas
a handful of baby spinach
½ tbsp hemp seeds
1 tbsp almond butter
1 small piece of ginger, peeled
½ a ripe avocado, peeled, stoned
    and roughly chopped
juice of ½ a lime
250ml almond milk

Simply put all the ingredients into a blender and blend until smooth and creamy. For a runnier consistency, add a little more almond milk.

Soothing Turmeric Tonic

Warming and comforting, this tonic is ideal when you feel slightly under the weather or you've had one too many drinks the night before. Turmeric has well-known anti-inflammatory benefits and skin-loving antioxidants. Lemon aids digestion and is bursting with vitamin C, essential for collagen production and a healthy immune system. This tonic is soothing and hydrating and it always does the trick to bring me back to life when I am not feeling myself.

SERVES 2

1 tbsp grated ginger
½ tbsp grated fresh turmeric
juice of 1 lemon
¼ tsp ground cinnamon
½ tsp vanilla bean paste
1–2 tbsp maple syrup

Put all the ingredients plus 600ml fresh water into a small pan on a medium to low heat. Allow the tonic to gently simmer for 4–5 minutes, then remove from the heat and strain through a small strainer set over a mug. Enjoy while still hot.

TIP
I would highly recommend using fresh ginger and turmeric. If you can't get your hands on them you can use 1 teaspoon of ground ginger and ½ teaspoon of ground turmeric.

Digestive Rooibos, Fennel & Ginger Infusion

I love sipping herbal teas and infusions throughout the day. It is the easiest way to keep your skin hydrated, with the additional health benefits of the herbs and spices. This rooibos infusion is one of my go-to caffeine-free teas. I have it multiple times a day, often with a dash of almond milk. It has a slight natural sweetness and is packed with polyphenols, including quercetin, rutin and ferulic acid, which give it strong antioxidant value. Pair it with some fennel seeds and ginger and you have a super skin-boosting, digestion-aiding infusion, amazing after a big meal or if you feel a bit sluggish.

SERVES 2

1 tbsp loose-leaf rooibos tea
½ tbsp fennel seeds
½ tbsp fresh grated ginger
½ tsp ground cinnamon
½ tsp vanilla bean paste
1–2 tbsp maple syrup, to sweeten (optional)
a dash of plant milk of your choice, to serve

Put 600ml fresh water into a small pan, add the roiboos tea, fennel seeds, ginger, cinnamon and vanilla and place on a medium heat. Bring to the boil, then turn the heat down to low and simmer gently for 8–10 minutes. Add the maple syrup (if using), stir everything together and remove from the heat.

Strain through a small strainer set over a mug. Add a dash of plant milk of your choice and enjoy while still hot.

Hibiscus Cold Brew

When most people think of hibiscus, thoughts of colourful flowers probably come to mind, and while it looks gorgeous in a tropical garden, it should also have a firm place in your beauty arsenal. Hibiscus offers a rich mix of plant compounds, including antioxidants, vitamins and minerals. It is particularly high in an antioxidant called myricetin. This compound is incredibly powerful in fighting collagen loss, which naturally occurs as we get older, and helps keep your skin plump and glowing. I use the steeping method for this infusion, which means I leave the dried hibiscus flowers in water overnight to release the flavour and nutrients. It offers all-day tea refreshment, and I serve it with plenty of ice during the summer for a flower power, natural thirst-quencher.

MAKES A 1-LITRE BOTTLE

20g dried hibiscus flowers
a thumb-size piece of ginger, cut into pieces
juice of 2 oranges

Put the dried hibiscus flowers and ginger into a 1-litre jar and fill the jar all the way to the top with boiling water. Leave it to cool down for 10–15 minutes, then cover the jar with a lid and let it steep overnight or for at least 8 hours.

Drain the tea through a strainer and pour it back into the jar with the orange juice. Drink as it is, or serve with lots of ice cubes.

Green Goddess Smoothie

This smoothie will really make you feel like a goddess or a god. It's super-nourishing and your skin will sing with joy at every sip. I try to have one of these every day, as it's the easiest and quickest way to cram in lots of skin-boosting minerals and antioxidants in one simple click of a button. The multitude of skin benefits in even just one serving of greens includes a hefty dose of vitamin A (a powerful skin smoother that prevents blemishes and fine lines), vitamin C (essential to boost collagen production) and vitamin K (which may be helpful to tackle dark circles). If you are new to green smoothies, start with a small handful of kale and slowly increase the amount as your taste buds adapt over time.

SERVES 1

2 frozen bananas
½ a cucumber
1 stick of celery
juice of ½ a lime
a thumb-size piece of ginger, peeled
a generous handful of
    chopped kale
1 heaped tbsp nut butter of
    your choice (I normally use
    almond butter)
1 tbsp hemp seeds

Simply put all the ingredients into a blender, along with 200ml fresh water, and blend until smooth and creamy. Add more water if you would like a runnier consistency.

Hydrating Strawberry & Coconut Lemonade

This refreshing lemonade is the ultimate drink after a sweaty workout. Coconut water is a great way to replenish the electrolytes lost during exercise. These include magnesium, potassium, sodium and calcium, and they are very important in maintaining fluid balance in the body. The strawberries add a delicious sweetness and a burst of collagen-promoting vitamin C, not in short supply thanks to the lime too!

SERVES 2

200g strawberries, trimmed
    and sliced + extra to serve
600ml coconut water
a handful of ice cubes
1 lime, thinly sliced

Put the strawberries into a blender with the coconut water and blend until smooth. Pour the strawberry water into a jug or large jar and add the ice cubes, lime slices and a few extra slices of strawberry. Stir everything together and pour into a glass to serve.

If you are drinking on-the-go, the best way to store this is in a bottle or insulated flask.

On-the-go Raspberry & Mint Chia Fresca

You might get a few looks when carrying around this undoubtedly weird-looking drink, but trust me, it's worth it, as it will guarantee you stay hydrated all day long in the most delicious way possible. Chia seeds, which swell into a gel-like consistency when they come in contact with water, are an excellent source of brain- and heart-boosting omega-3 fatty acids and are also great in lowering inflammation and plumping the skin. I love the addition of raspberry and mint, which make this fresca even more refreshing.

SERVES 1

300ml coconut water
50g fresh or frozen raspberries
1 tbsp chia seeds
a few fresh mint leaves

Put the coconut water and raspberries into a blender and blend until smooth. Pour into your glass bottle or jar. Add the chia seeds and mint leaves. Put on the lid and shake everything together to make sure the chia seeds don't clump together.

Let the fresca sit in the fridge for 15 minutes before drinking. The best way to drink it is out of a jar or a bottle, so you can put a cap on and shake it up. The chia seeds will naturally sink to the bottom of the bottle.

Pick-me-up Caramel & Apple Smoothie

This smoothie tastes utterly decadent and it's the perfect sweet afternoon pick-me-up. I absolutely love the caramel notes of the Medjool date combined with the apple and banana. You honestly won't believe that something so healthy can taste so indulgent! Packed with fibre, protein, healthy fats and wholefoods, this smoothie is a winning healthy treat or post-workout snack.

SERVES 1

1 frozen banana
1 apple, core and seeds removed
1 Medjool date, pitted
1 tbsp almond butter
½ tbsp ground flaxseeds
½ tsp ground cinnamon + extra for dusting
  (optional)
300ml almond milk, to blend

Simply put all the ingredients into a blender and blend until smooth and creamy. Serve with a dusting of ground cinnamon, if you like.

Sleepy Cashew Milk

During the colder months, there is nothing I love more than curling up on the sofa with a piping hot drink to relax after a long day. Hot cacao can be magical but I find it too energizing for the evenings. This sleepy cashew milk hits the right note before bedtime, as I always find it very soothing and calming. The antioxidant-rich array of spices in this creamy cashew drink supports glowing skin and restful sleep. Cashews are also a wonderful source of zinc, which has antibacterial properties to help fight breakouts. The combination of warming spices and creamy homemade cashew milk makes this a really special, toasty treat.

SERVES 2

100g raw cashews, soaked in
    boiling water for 30 minutes
2 cardamom pods
1 tsp vanilla bean paste
1 tsp ground cinnamon
½–1 tsp ground ginger
    (depending on how spicy
    you like it)
¼ tsp ground nutmeg
2 Medjool dates, pitted

Drain the cashews, then put them into a food processor with 700ml of fresh water and blend until smooth and frothy. Pour the milk through a nut milk bag, a cheesecloth or a clean cotton tea towel, squeezing all the milk out of the bag as you go.

Discard the nut pulp or use it for another recipe (see Tip below) and pour the milk into a pan. Give the blender a quick rinse. Bash the cardamom pods and remove the seeds. Add the cardamom seeds and all the other ingredients to the milk and mix well. Set the pan of milk on a medium heat and allow to heat gently, about 2–3 minutes. Pour the milk back into the blender and blend until the dates have dissolved and the milk has a silky consistency. Pour into a mug and enjoy while hot.

TIPS
If you are pressed for time, use your favourite shop-bought dairy-free milk: I recommend cashew or coconut. If you've made your own, try adding the nut pulp to porridge, smoothies or energy balls.

Wake-me-up Cacao Elixir

If you fancy something a bit different to coffee but with that same energizing element, this elixir with date and cinnamon is subtly sweet and heavenly delicious. Raw cacao contains many natural chemicals, including beneficial flavonoids, plant compounds which have antioxidant properties that help prevent cell damage and slow down the signs of ageing. This is also a great drink if you crave something sweet after a meal and don't want to make or eat a big dessert.

SERVE 2

100g raw cashews soaked in
    boiling water for 30 minutes
2 tbsp raw cacao powder
½ tsp ground cinnamon
1 tsp vanilla bean paste
1 tbsp almond butter
2 Medjool dates, pitted

Drain the cashews, then put them into a food processor with 600ml of fresh water. Blend until smooth and frothy. Pour the milk through a nut milk bag, a cheesecloth or a clean cotton tea towel, squeezing all the milk out of the bag as you go.

Discard the nut pulp or use it for another recipe (see Tip on page 200) and pour the milk into a pan on a medium heat. Give the blender a quick rinse. Add the rest of the ingredients to the milk and mix well. Allow the milk to heat gently, about 2–3 minutes, then pour the milk back into the blender and blend until the dates have dissolved and the milk has a silky consistency. Pour into a mug and enjoy while hot.

Snacks

I don't know about you, but I am a serial snacker. When I started to make changes to my diet, one of the things I struggled with was finding healthy and nutrient-dense snacks. I believe it is crucial to have healthy snacks in your kitchen so that you always have something nutritious to enjoy, to stop you reaching for the ultra-processed stuff.

"Homemade snacks are crucial to keep my mood stable and help to stave off any cravings."

Although these days more healthy options are widely available, I still prefer to make my own snacks and treats. First and foremost, I want complete control over every ingredient used, but I also take a lot of pleasure from the creative process involved in concocting my very own Happy Skin Kitchen super-snack cabinet.

All the recipes in this chapter are really easy to make, and most of them keep for a while, so you can stock up your pantry, cupboards and fridge with snacks to keep you energized at all times. They're great at home, at the desk or even if, like me, you're a bit of a globetrotter. Some of the show-stopping snacks that you will often find in my handbag include my Savoury Carrot & Sun-dried Tomato Muffins, Raw Brownie Protein Bars and Quinoa & Cacao Power Balls. The ultimate afternoon pick-me-ups, working perfectly to boost our energy levels, this tasty trio is crucial in keeping my mood stable and helping to stave off any cravings. This is because they are packed with healthy fats, plant-based protein and fibre. Protein is so important for keeping you energized and feeling fuller for longer. The more fibre something contains, the slower it is released into your bloodstream, so it also helps to keep you satiated. You will stay satisfied for longer, and rather than your blood sugar levels rocketing up and down, they will stay balanced and hunger pangs will be a thing of the past! I would recommend keeping some of these snacks in your desk at work, or in your bag while you're on the move. Most of these snacks are also freezer-friendly, which means you only need to make a batch once and then they are good to be stored in the freezer for months. For example, I love to make my Nutrient-dense Bread and store it in a sealable food bag in the freezer already sliced. All I have to do is pop a slice in the toaster, spread over a dollop of almond butter and load it with sliced banana. In less than 5 minutes, I have a wholesome and delicious pick-me-up.

Banana & Peanut Butter Bites

These are the epitome of a healthy and simple snack. They are sweetened only by the ripe bananas and they have a scrumptious, soft and chewy texture. The peanut butter and chocolate chips add a lovely richness, which goes so well with the sweet banana and coconut. Bananas are a complex carb, so they are great for sustained energy, and they also contain silicon, an essential element for strong hair, nails and collagen. These are the perfect afternoon snack, sweet but not overly indulgent or sickly, and full of fibre to keep you motoring until dinner time.

MAKES 10–13 BITES,
DEPENDING ON THE SIZE

160g very ripe bananas
   (about 2 small ones)
70g porridge oats
40g desiccated coconut
4 tbsp runny peanut butter
½ tsp vanilla bean paste
40g dark chocolate chips

Preheat the oven to 200°C/180°C fan/gas 6 and line a baking tray with parchment paper.

Put the bananas into a large bowl and mash them with a fork. Add the porridge oats, desiccated coconut, peanut butter, vanilla bean paste and chocolate chips. Mix everything together until all the ingredients are combined. Using an ice cream scoop or your hands (make sure you wet them to prevent everything sticking), shape the dough into round cookies and place them on the lined baking tray.

Bake in the oven for 17 minutes, then remove and let them cool down for just a few minutes. They are delicious cold or warm.

Fruity Flapjacks

I have been obsessed with these flapjacks since the first time I made them. They just tick all the boxes: chewy, fruity and naturally sweet with a hint of cacao. To sweeten them, I use a combination of dates, apricots and raisins, which also works to bind the mixture together and at the same time adds fibre, beauty minerals and vitamins. Dried apricots, for example, are a great source of many antioxidants, including beta-carotene and vitamins E, C, and A. They help to protect your skin against UV damage and environmental pollutants by neutralizing free radicals. I have added walnuts not just for their moreish flavour but because they also provide healthy omega-3 fatty acids that strengthen the membranes of your skin cells, locking in moisture and nutrients to keep your skin plump, glowing and protect against toxins.

These flapjacks are a sensational sweet afternoon pick-me-up, but to make them a little more indulgent, drizzle over some melted dark chocolate.

MAKES 12 X 6CM FLAPJACKS

150g pitted dates
100g dried apricots
4 tbsp melted coconut oil
1 tsp vanilla bean paste
150g porridge oats
50g walnuts
30g sunflower seeds
50g raisins
20g cacao nibs
70g good quality dark
    chocolate to drizzle on top
    (optional) (I love to use
    70–80% cocoa)

Put the pitted dates and the apricots into a large heatproof bowl. Cover with boiling water and leave to soak for 10 minutes.

Preheat the oven to 200°C/180°C fan/gas 6 and line a 20cm square brownie tin with parchment paper.

Drain the soaked dates and apricots and put them into a food processor with the melted coconut oil and vanilla bean paste. Blitz until you have a chunky sticky paste, then add the oats, walnuts, sunflower seeds and raisins and blitz again until you have a sticky dough. Add the cacao nibs and pulse a few times until they are incorporated into the mixture.

Spread the mixture evenly in the brownie tin and bake for 20 minutes, until slightly golden around the edges. Then remove from the oven and let the flapjack cool completely in the tin.

In the meantime, melt the dark chocolate (if using) by placing it in a heatproof bowl over a small pan of water on a low heat until smooth. Remove the flapjack from the tin but leave it on the baking paper. Drizzle the melted chocolate on top. Leave the chocolate to set at room temperature, then cut the flapjack into bars.

Store in an airtight container at room temperature for up to 3–5 days.

Quinoa & Cacao Power Balls

I know adding cooked quinoa to a sweet recipe might sound a bit odd, but it actually works wonderfully well, much better than I originally anticipated! The moisture from the quinoa together with the dates makes these bliss balls incredibly gooey and fudgy. And if you are not the biggest fan of this pseudo-grain, don't worry – you really won't taste it! I have been making these on repeat since I mastered the recipe, as they are decadently chocolatey and yet so incredibly healthy. They are the perfect bite when hunger strikes, and they are guaranteed to keep you feeling full and satiated for hours. The quinoa not only brings in a dose of plant-based protein but it is also high in fibre, minerals and skin-loving antioxidants, which are already not in short supply thanks to the mighty raw cacao. The ground almonds and nut butter add a delicious buttery texture and a boost of healthy fats and vitamin E, the beauty vitamin that keeps your skin hydrated and helps protect it from the sun.

MAKES 10 BALLS

50g ground almonds
70g cooked quinoa
30g porridge oats
2 tbsp raw cacao powder
60g pitted Medjool dates
1 tbsp nut butter of your choice
(I have used almond)
½ tsp vanilla bean paste

Put the ground almonds, cooked quinoa, oats and raw cacao powder into a food processor, and blitz until you have a fine crumbly consistency. Add the pitted dates, nut butter and vanilla bean paste and blitz again until the mixture sticks together when you press it between your fingers. Roll the dough into small balls. Enjoy straight away, or either store them in an airtight container in the fridge for 3–4 days, or freeze for up to 2–3 months.

Coconut & Vanilla Chia Pudding with Berry Compote

I am a big fan of chia puddings, as they are super quick to make and they are perfect for a light breakfast, snack or even dessert. The secret to making them super-creamy and sweet without the addition of any refined sugar is to use coconut yogurt and coconut milk, as these two ingredients are naturally sweet, and of course endlessly creamy. By using these two together you create a really decadent and indulgent pudding-like consistency that nobody will ever guess is healthy too! Chia seeds are a powerhouse of nutrition. They are high in protein, iron, calcium and omega-3 fatty acids to help keep inflammation at bay, and are packed with soluble fibre, which ensures regular bowel movements and keeps you feeling fuller for longer. You can have the chia pudding as it is but I like to serve it with my spiced berry compote for a fruity taste explosion and a good dose of antioxidants.

SERVES 2

200ml coconut milk (from
  a carton)
25g unsweetened coconut yogurt
1 tsp vanilla bean paste
50g chia seeds

FOR THE BERRY COMPOTE:

frozen or fresh berries of your
  choice (I have used frozen
  raspberries)
1 cardamom pod, split open
  and seeds ground
1 tbsp maple syrup (optional)

TO SERVE:

handful of fresh raspberries
desiccated coconut, for sprinkling

In a large bowl mix together the coconut milk, coconut yogurt and vanilla bean paste. Add the chia seeds and then, using a whisk, mix everything together. Leave it to thicken to a gel-like consistency for 10 minutes, then mix again to prevent any lumps. Cover and place in the fridge to set for at least 3 hours or ideally overnight.

To make the berry compote, put all the berries into a large pan on a low heat together with the ground cardamom seeds and a splash of water. Simmer for 15–20 minutes, until the berries have a jam-like consistency. If using, stir through the maple syrup. Remove from the heat and set aside to cool down. The compote will thicken up even more once cold.

Divide the chia pudding between glasses or bowls and serve it with the berry compote on top, finishing each serving with fresh raspberries and desiccated coconut.

Bon Bon Dates Three Ways

When I started to move away from refined sugar these were the first treats I made, and I was honestly in disbelief that something so wholesome could taste so decadent. If you are trying to stay away from overly processed, high in refined sugary sweets but you still want a treat that feels indulgent, these are for you. I promise, once you make them you are not going to reach for sugary sweets any more. The non-negotiable ingredient you need is Medjool dates. I am afraid regular dates won't cut it. Medjool dates are irresistibly gooey and soft, with the most incredible caramel flavour. Although dates are undoubtedly high in fructose, they also pack in fibre, which helps with gut health and stabilizing blood sugar. They also have small amounts of iron, calcium, potassium and B vitamins. Below and overleaf you will find three different versions of this skin-friendly treat, which I have been making for years – I am confident you will love them as much as I do!

MAKES 7-8 DATES

70g good quality dark chocolate (I used 75% cocoa), broken into pieces
7–8 Medjool dates
40g almond butter
chopped nuts of your choice, freeze-dried raspberries or desiccated coconut, to decorate (optional)

ALMOND BUTTER & CHOCOLATE

This is the first version of stuffed dates I ever made, and is still one that I make time and time again. You just can't go wrong with silky almond butter and rich dark chocolate. These are pretty incredible as they are, but feel free to make them prettier by decorating them with sprinkles of your choice.

Desiccated coconut, chopped pistachios or freeze-dried raspberries will always give them a bit of extra glitz.

Melt the chocolate in a heatproof bowl over a pan of simmering water.

Slice open your dates and remove the pits. Generously stuff your dates with the almond butter. Line a plate or tray with parchment paper. Dip the stuffed dates into the melted chocolate until they are evenly coated. Place them on the lined plate or tray.

Garnish each date with sprinkles of your choice (if using) and transfer them to the fridge to set for 10–25 minutes. Store in the fridge in a covered container for up to 10 days, or in the freezer for a few months. Remove from the freezer 10–15 minutes before serving.

COOKIE DOUGH

The beauty of this filling is that it takes only 5 minutes and a tiny bit of mixing. The nutty, gooey and soft filling is perfectly balanced by the crunchy chocolate chunks. A little piece of heaven with every bite! I use cashew butter for its biscuit-like flavour, but any nut butter of your choice will work too.

MAKES 7–8 DATES

30g ground almonds
1½ tbsp cashew butter
½ tsp vanilla bean paste
½ tbsp oat milk
20g good quality dark chocolate
    (I love to use 70% cocoa), chopped
    into small pieces
7–8 Medjool dates

In a small bowl mix together the ground almonds, cashew butter, vanilla bean paste and oat milk. Once it is all well combined, stir through the chocolate chunks.

Slice open your dates and remove the pits. Generously stuff each date with the cookie dough filling. Store in the fridge in a covered container for up to 10 days, or in the freezer for few months. Remove from the freezer 10–15 minutes before serving.

PEANUT BUTTER & JELLY

Creamy peanut butter and tart raspberry jam has quickly become my new favourite filling. The sharpness of raspberries goes well with the richness of the peanut butter and the sweetness of the dates – it is truly a winning combination. If by any chance you have any raspberry jam left over, store it in an airtight container in the fridge for a few days. It's great with porridge, Bircher muesli or on toast.

MAKES 7–8 DATES

80g fresh or frozen raspberries
½ tsp chia seeds
½ tsp vanilla bean paste
7–8 Medjool dates
40g smooth or crunchy peanut butter
    (I love crunchy for this recipe)

Put the raspberries into a small pan and add a dash of water. Cook on a medium heat for about 10 minutes, until the raspberries start to fall apart. Add the chia seeds and vanilla bean paste. Stir everything together and cook for another 5 minutes, until you have a thick jam-like consistency. Remove from the heat and leave to cool.

Slice open your dates and remove the pits. Generously stuff your dates with peanut butter and top them with a little dollop of the raspberry jam.

If you are not serving these immediately, I would recommend that you only stuff them with the peanut butter and keep the jam stored in the fridge in an airtight container. The stuffed dates will store well for up to 10 days, the raspberry jam for 5 days.

Rosemary & Fennel Buckwheat Crackers

Shop-bought crackers usually leave a lot to be desired. This recipe is far more wholesome and nutrient dense, with fibre, minerals, vitamins and healthy fats. The buckwheat has a lower glycaemic index than wheat flour and high levels of iron, magnesium and protein, and works really well with chickpea flour. Packing in plenty of nutrition, the mix is rich in zinc, which has anti-inflammatory properties, essential to fight breakouts and acne. Both flours are also very high in fibre, to keep you feeling fuller for longer, and will feed your gut microbiome at the same time, resulting in better digestion and glowing skin! The combination of the fennel seeds and rosemary is delightful and it's also a great way to add lots of extra antioxidants and minerals. Serve these with my Kale Pesto Dip (page 246) for a nourishing snack that your skin will thank you for!

MAKES AROUND 50 SMALL CRACKERS

2 tsp fennel seeds
220g buckwheat flour + extra
    for dusting
50g chickpea flour (also called
    gram flour)
2 tbsp dried rosemary
2 tsp sea salt + extra to sprinkle
    on top
a generous twist of black pepper
60ml extra virgin olive oil
100ml cold water

Preheat the oven to 220°C/200°C fan/gas 7 and line two large baking trays with parchment paper.

Put the fennel seeds into a dry pan and toast them for few minutes on a medium heat until fragrant. Using a pestle and mortar, roughly crush them.

In a large bowl, mix together the buckwheat flour, chickpea flour, rosemary, sea salt, crushed fennel seed and black pepper. Pour in the extra virgin olive oil and water. Start mixing with a spoon, and when the dough begins to come together, using your hands, knead it into a ball.

Dust your working surface with a little buckwheat flour. Cut the dough into 4 balls. Using a rolling pin and working one ball at the time, stretch the dough Into a flat rectangular shape. Make sure you roll it out very thinly. Using a sharp knife, cut out long rectangular crackers, about 5cm wide, then cut them into squares. Don't worry if they look a bit wonky – they will still be tasty.

Transfer the crackers to the baking trays. Sprinkle them with sea salt and bake in the oven for 12 minutes, until golden brown around the edges. Remove from the oven and allow to cool completely.

Store the crackers in an airtight container for up to 3 weeks.

Cacao Nib & Hazelnut Bites

The first time I baked these bites, I ate half of them in less than 5 minutes. That's how good they are! They are little morsels of joy – nutty, slightly crumbly, with chewy sweetness from the dried apricots and rich bitterness from the cacao nibs. You might want to make a double batch, because I promise you, they won't last very long.

Hazelnuts are not just utterly delicious but they provide a good dose of vitamin E, an important beauty vitamin to help protect the skin against UV rays. Cacao nibs (where chocolate comes from) are a powerhouse of antioxidants, containing even more than blueberries! Cacao nibs also contain flavonoids, anti-inflammatory antioxidants that help protect the heart and the arteries in your heart and brain. And as if that wasn't enough, they are also rich in polyphenols that help protect cells from oxidation, keeping your skin looking youthful. I love serving them with a cup of my Soothing Turmeric Tonic (page 192) for a blissful afternoon break.

MAKES ABOUT 12 BITES

110g ground hazelnuts
40g oat flour
½ tsp baking powder
½ tsp bicarbonate of soda
1 tbsp cacao nibs
a pinch of sea salt
1 tbsp melted coconut oil
2 tbsp maple syrup
1 tbsp runny almond butter
2 tbsp plant milk of your choice
   (I have used oat)
1 tsp vanilla bean paste
40g dried apricots, finely chopped

Preheat the oven to 200°C/180°C fan/gas 6 and line a baking tray with parchment paper.

In a large bowl, mix together the ground hazelnuts, oat flour, baking powder, bicarbonate of soda, cacao nibs and sea salt.

In a separate bowl mix together the melted coconut oil, maple syrup, almond butter, plant milk and vanilla bean paste. Add the wet ingredients to the dry and fold in the chopped apricots. Mix well until you have a sticky cookie dough. Wet your hands slightly (so the mixture won't stick) and roll the cookie mixture into about 12 small balls. Place them on the baking tray and flatten them slightly – you want macaroon kind of size.

Bake in the oven for 10 minutes, until the bites are golden brown around the edges. Remove from the oven and let them cool down on the tray.

Raw Brownie Protein Bars

I love making a batch of these and storing them in the freezer so I know I always have a delicious and nourishing treat on hand. They are a great snack to pack with me if I am on the go or after a sweaty workout. The prominent source of protein in these chocolatey bars is hemp seeds, a tiny but mighty seed that really packs a nutritious punch. Hemp seeds are not only a complete protein source, which means they provide all the essential amino acids, but they are also rich in anti-inflammatory omega-3 fatty acids including gamma-linolenic acids, important fatty acids for healthy skin and for helping with skin conditions such as eczema. They are also a great source of vitamin E, another vital beauty mineral, and zinc, which helps fight breakouts.

These bars are not just a powerhouse of nutrition but they also taste like chocolate brownies, thanks to the roasted hazelnuts, which when blended together with the dates and raw cacao powder, create the most decadent combination. I add dark chocolate chunks for extra richness, but they will still be lovely, even without.

MAKES 16 X 5CM BARS

150g hazelnuts
300g pitted dates
50g raisins
2 tbsp nut butter of your choice
   (I have used almond)
1 tsp vanilla bean paste
100g buckwheat grains
100g hemp seeds
4 tbsp raw cacao powder
60g dark chocolate, roughly
   chopped (optional) (I love
   to use 70–80% cocoa)

FOR THE TOPPING:
70g good quality dark chocolate,
   roughly chopped (optional)
   (I love to use 70–80% cocoa)
sea salt flakes

Preheat the oven to 200°C/180°C fan/gas 6 and line a 20cm square brownie tin with parchment paper.

Put the hazelnuts on a large baking tray and roast in the oven for 10 minutes, until they are golden brown. Remove from the oven and let them cool down for 10–15 minutes.

Put the dates and raisins into a food processor together with the nut butter and vanilla bean paste. Blitz everything together until you have a chunky, sticky paste. Add the roasted hazelnuts, buckwheat grains, hemp seeds and raw cacao, and pulse a few times until you have a sticky dough. Add the dark chocolate pieces (if using) and pulse a few times, just so they are incorporated in the dough.

Melt the chocolate for the topping (if using) in a heatproof bowl over a small pan of simmering water on a low heat.

Spread the brownie mixture in the lined brownie tin and press it down using the back of a spoon, until it's evenly distributed. Drizzle the melted chocolate on top. Place the tin in the freezer for 1 hour to set.

Remove from the freezer, sprinkle with sea salt flakes and cut into rectangles. Store them in the fridge for up to 2 weeks, or in the freezer for 2–3 months.

Savoury Carrot & Sun-dried Tomato Muffins

These muffins are surprisingly light and fluffy, and they are a big obsession of mine. They are the best handbag snack, lunchbox addition, flight survival treat, and a great all-round alternative to bread. For this recipe I use chickpea flour, which tastes delicious in savoury dishes and is also a powerhouse of nutrients and minerals, high in fibre and protein. Chickpeas are a brilliant source of magnesium and copper, both key in promoting skin elasticity. They are also rich in zinc, a very important beauty mineral to help keep breakouts at bay.

These muffins are also a fab way to squeeze extra vegetables into your diet, and carrots are a wonderful source of beta-carotene, which our body converts into vitamin A, one of the most essential vitamins to help prevent premature ageing. The Mediterranean herbs, nutritional yeast and sun-dried tomatoes add so much flavour, making these muffins so moreish and scrumptious that you will want to make them over and over again!

MAKES 12 MUFFINS

180g chickpea flour (also called gram flour)
40g buckwheat flour
30g nutritional yeast
1 tsp baking powder
1 tsp bicarbonate of soda
1 tsp smoked paprika
1 tbsp dried oregano
1 tsp ground turmeric
1 tsp salt
a twist of black pepper
400ml oat milk
2 tbsp extra virgin olive oil
30g pitted olives (I have used Kalamata), finely chopped
40g sun-dried tomatoes, finely chopped
2 medium carrots, finely grated

Preheat the oven to 200°C/180°C fan/gas 6 and line a 12-hole muffin tray with muffin cases.

In a large bowl, mix together the chickpea flour, buckwheat flour, nutritional yeast, baking powder, bicarbonate of soda, smoked paprika, oregano, turmeric, salt and pepper.

In a separate bowl, mix the oat milk with the olive oil, chopped olives, sun-dried tomatoes and grated carrots. Pour the wet ingredients into the dry and gently combine everything together until you don't see any more dry flour.

Place about 3 tablespoons of the mixture in each muffin case, and bake in the oven for 30 minutes, until risen and golden brown on top. Remove from the oven and let the muffins cool down in the tray for 10 minutes, then transfer them to a rack to cool down completely.

Store the muffins in an airtight container at room temperature for up to 2–3 days.

TIP
These muffins are suitable for freezing, so are great for weekly meal prep. Remove from the freezer and place them in the oven for 10 minutes, until warm right through.

Nutrient-dense Bread

Don't get me wrong, I love buying a loaf of soft bread with a crunchy crust as much as the next person, but when you can create a bake like this nutrient-dense bread, you will honestly think twice. As the name suggests, it's truly loaded with nutrition and nourishment that your skin and your body will thank you for. Buckwheat is supercharged with B complex vitamins including thiamin (B1), riboflavin (B2), niacin (B3), pantothenic acid (B5), pyridoxine (B6) and folate (B9). These vitamins work both synergistically and individually to promote healthy skin and strong hair. In addition, the rutin in buckwheat has strong antioxidant properties, which can help keep premature wrinkles at bay. Thanks to the array of different seeds, this bread will also boost your intake of healthy fats and omega-3. Flaxseeds, for example, contain lignans and antioxidants that help in the prevention of fine lines. Also, the fatty acids in flax seeds help in keeping your skin hydrated and plump.

MAKES 1 LOAF

400g buckwheat grains, soaked overnight
65g quinoa, soaked overnight
2 tbsp chia seeds
2 tbsp ground flaxseeds
2 tbsp extra virgin olive oil
1 tbsp maple syrup
2 tsp apple cider vinegar
1 tsp bicarbonate of soda
1 tsp sea salt
60g oat flour
65g pumpkin seeds + extra for sprinkling on top (optional)
65g sunflower seeds + extra for sprinkling on top (optional)

Preheat the oven to 180°C/160°C fan/gas 4 and line a 23 x 13cm loaf tin with parchment paper.

Drain and rinse the soaked buckwheat grains. Make sure you rinse them thoroughly, to eliminate all the slimy water that the buckwheat naturally produces when soaked. Drain and rinse the quinoa as well. Put both of these into a food processor and blitz until you have a porridge kind of consistency. If your food processor is not big enough, you can do this in batches.

Pour the mixture into a large bowl and add 250ml of cold water, the chia seeds, ground flaxseeds, extra virgin olive oil, maple syrup, apple cider vinegar, bicarbonate of soda and sea salt. Mix everything together until well combined, then let the batter sit for 15 minutes until it has thickened slightly. Add the oat flour, pumpkin seeds and sunflower seeds, and mix well. Pour the mixture into the loaf tin and spread it evenly. Sprinkle the top with extra sunflower and pumpkin seeds, if you like, and bake in the oven for 2 hours. A toothpick inserted into the loaf should come out clean.

Remove from the oven and let the loaf sit in the tin for 15 minutes, then transfer it to a rack and allow it to cool down completely, ideally overnight or for at least 3–4 hours.

The loaf will keep for up to a week, stored in an airtight bag in the fridge. Alternatively, slice it and store it in the freezer for up to 3 months.

Dips & Sides

I confess I have an addiction to dips
and side dishes. This is probably
one of my favourite chapters in the
book, as there is such a wide range
of ingredients, flavour combinations
and textures to play around with.

"These recipes are an easy way to incorporate more plant-diversity into your diet."

These delicious dips and salubrious sides are wonderful on their own or when used as sidekicks to showstopping mains, but throw two or three together and you've got yourself a hearty bowl of bliss. The recipes in this chapter are my most cherished creations, the kind of dishes I make week-in and week-out. The Harissa Sweet Potatoes with Roasted Garlic & Tahini Dressing, Curried Greens and Broccoli & Quinoa Tabbouleh are all absolute winners, and I have a feeling they could become superstar staples in your diet too. They are all effortless to make and most can be made in advance, to take pride of place in any lunchbox. These recipes can also be mixed and matched with just about anything, so if you are not yet the biggest vegetable eater, you can just add these to your existing on-the-go meals. That way, you can experiment with new ingredients and gradually introduce more plant-based foods without it all feeling too overwhelming.

The dips, in particular, are fabulous for fortifying your meals with minimum effort. I make creamy dips using nuts, seeds, lentils, beans and vegetables. I particularly love using roasted vegetables such as pepper and cauliflower, but you can really use up any veg that you have lying around in the fridge, making it a brilliant way of reducing food waste. An exceptional dip gives bags of extra flavour and nourishment to any salad, plus they are also amazing accompaniments to my Happy Skin bowls. With the right dip I can happily munch on vegetables all day! Try my smoky Pepper and Sun-dried Tomato Dip with some sliced crudités for a filling and antioxidant-packed snack.

All the dips in this chapter are thick, creamy and make a beautiful sharing spread if you have friends over. I often serve them with my Rosemary & Fennel Buckwheat Crackers (page 219). They all store well in the fridge for 3 or 4 days, so I often make one of them at the beginning of the week, then if I am pressed for time I can just spread it over a slice of bread for a speedy breakfast or lunch. Finally, if you are a meat eater, these are an easy way to incorporate more plant diversity into your diet and give you an insight into how lip-smackingly tasty vegetables can be!

Shaved Brussels Sprouts, Butternut & Hazelnut Salad

I know some people don't even like cooked Brussels sprouts, so the idea of eating them raw may seem madness, but trust me – this salad is unexpectedly delicious and moreish. The natural bitterness and sturdy leaves of the sprouts are perfectly balanced by the sweetness of the roasted butternut squash, apple and pomegranate. Brussels sprouts are rich in vitamin C (especially when eaten raw, as vitamin C is heat sensitive), sulphorane and antioxidants. This magic trio helps the body fight viral infections, and they have also been shown to have anti-cancer properties. The high concentration of vitamin C is key to supporting collagen production, which creates better skin elasticity and prevents premature ageing. The addition of butternut squash is a skin match made in heaven, as it brings to the table one of my favourite antioxidants – beta-carotene – which serves to protect the proteins in our skin that keep it supple and youthful. The creamy tahini dressing is what really brings this salad together, adding a delicious creaminess, plus skin-loving fats, and calcium to help keep your nails strong and healthy.

SERVES 2

3 tbsp extra virgin olive oil + extra
    for drizzling
3 tbsp red wine vinegar
2 garlic cloves, crushed
½ tsp Dijon mustard
½ tbsp maple syrup
a few sprigs of fresh thyme
250g Brussels sprouts, trimmed
    and finely shredded
500g butternut squash, peeled
    and cut into cubes
1 tsp smoked paprika
60g hazelnuts
seeds of ½ a pomegranate
½ an apple, cut into thin
    matchstick slices
salt and pepper, to taste

FOR THE TAHINI DRESSING:

3 tbsp runny tahini
2 tsp red wine vinegar
1 tsp white miso paste
1 tsp maple syrup
1 tbsp lemon juice

Preheat the oven to 220°C/200°C fan/gas 7.

Put the extra virgin olive oil, red wine vinegar, crushed garlic, Dijon mustard, maple syrup and fresh thyme into a large bowl and mix everything together. Add the shredded Brussels sprouts and toss them in the dressing. Let the Brussels sprouts marinate while you are making the rest of the dish.

Put the butternut squash on a large baking tray, drizzle with olive oil, and sprinkle with salt, pepper and the smoked paprika. Mix everything together and roast in the oven for 25 minutes. Remove the tray from the oven, make a little space on the tray and add the hazelnuts. Put the tray back into the oven for 5 more minutes, until the hazelnuts are golden brown.

While the butternut squash is roasting, make the tahini dressing by simply whisking together all the ingredients and adding 2 or 3 tablespoons of cold water to thin it out.

To assemble the salad, add the sliced apple to the Brussels sprouts together with the roasted butternut squash. Sprinkle the pomegranate seeds and hazelnuts on top and drizzle with the tahini dressing.

Harissa Sweet Potatoes with Roasted Garlic & Tahini Dressing

Harissa paste is one of those ingredients that instantly makes anything taste better. I always have a jar in the fridge, as it's an amazing addition to lots of different meals. It's out of this world in this recipe, as its warm and fiery spices go so well with the natural sweetness of the sweet potatoes.

Sweet potatoes are known for having high levels of beta-carotene, which is converted to an active form of vitamin A by our body. Vitamin A is required for cell production and growth. Anthocyanins are another antioxidant abundant in sweet potatoes.

The creamy roasted garlic, tahini and coconut yogurt dressing is what lifts these sweet potatoes to magnificence. I have been utterly devoted to this dish since the first time I made it. The coriander and spring onions add a delicious zingy burst of freshness, so please don't skip them!

SERVES 4 AS A SIDE

1kg sweet potatoes (skin on),
   cut into chunks
3 tbsp harissa paste

FOR THE DRESSING:
1 head of garlic
3 tbsp plain coconut yogurt
2 tbsp runny tahini
1 tbsp lemon juice
½ tbsp extra virgin olive oil
1 tsp maple syrup
salt and pepper, to taste

SERVE WITH:
2 spring onions, finely sliced
a handful of chopped fresh
   coriander
chilli flakes (optional)

Preheat the oven to 220°C/200°C fan/gas 7.

Put the chopped sweet potatoes on a large baking tray. Add the harissa paste and toss everything together. Slice the top off the garlic head and add it to the tray.

Cover the tray with some kitchen foil and put it into the oven for 30 minutes. Remove the foil and return the tray to the oven for 15–20 more minutes, until the sweet potatoes are soft and slightly crispy around the edges.

Remove the garlic head and squeeze the flesh out of the skin. Put the roasted garlic into a blender with the coconut yogurt, tahini, lemon juice, extra virgin olive oil, maple syrup and a generous pinch each of salt and pepper. Blend until smooth and creamy.

Put the roasted sweet potatoes on a large platter and drizzle with the roasted garlic dressing. Serve scattered with the sliced spring onions and fresh coriander, and a sprinkling of chilli flakes (if you like).

Curried Greens

I am always looking for different ways of cooking leafy greens, as they have become such a staple in my diet. Leafy greens such as collard greens, kale and chard are truly some of the most nutrient-dense foods on the planet. They not only have high vitamin A content, which is essential for the growth of all bodily tissues, including skin and hair, but they are also brimming with vitamin C, which is a fundamental beauty vitamin. Collard greens tend to have quite a bitter flavour, and that's why I love this recipe so much, because the coconut milk and warm spices really transform them into something delicious.

I usually have these as a side for my Black Dhal (page 136) but they are also lovely served with roasted root vegetables.

SERVES 2

1 tbsp melted coconut oil
2 shallots, finely chopped
2 garlic cloves, crushed
a thumb-size piece of ginger, peeled and grated
2 red bird's-eye chillies, finely chopped
1 tbsp curry powder
200g mixed leafy greens, such as collard greens, Savoy cabbage and cavolo nero, stems removed and leaves thinly chopped
½ x 400ml tin of coconut milk
100g frozen peas
½ tbsp coconut sugar
1 tbsp tamari sauce

Put the coconut oil into a large frying pan on a medium heat. Once hot, add the shallots and cook for 5–8 minutes, until the shallots start to caramelize.

Add the crushed garlic, ginger, chillies and curry powder. Stir everything together and cook for 1–2 more minutes, until the spices are fragrant.

Add the greens and pour over the coconut milk. Mix everything together so the greens are coated in the spices and cook for 10 minutes. Add the frozen peas, stir everything together and cook for another 5–8 minutes, until the greens are soft but still have bite. I like mine quite al dente but if you prefer yours a bit softer, cook them for another 5 minutes.

Season with the coconut sugar and tamari sauce, mix everything together and serve while still hot.

Root Veggie Crumble

This is one of those recipes that turned out to be such a revelation. I was definitely a bit sceptical about the idea of a savoury veggie crumble, but it absolutely works! It's also a fun way to spruce up your humble root vegetables. The mix of oats, buttery walnuts and pecans with the warm spices creates the most sensational crunchy topping, which makes this dish an absolute joy to eat. Although celeriac isn't a very popular vegetable, it is actually a nutritional powerhouse, packed with skin-boosting antioxidants, vitamins B6, C and K. I love it with the nutty crumble topping, which also adds plenty of healthy fats and minerals to help keep your skin supple and glowing.

   Although this is a side dish, I love to also serve it as a main on a thick layer of my coconut and tahini whip, which makes this recipe even more irresistible.

SERVES 4 AS A SIDE

2 medium carrots, cut
    into cubes
2 medium beetroots, peeled
    and cut into cubes
300g celeriac, peeled and
    cut into cubes
a drizzle of olive oil, for roasting
salt and pepper, to taste

FOR THE CRUMBLE:

1 tbsp fennel seeds
1 tbsp cumin seeds
40g walnuts, roughly chopped
40g pecans, roughly chopped
40g rolled oats
20g pumpkin seeds
1 tbsp sesame seeds
1 tsp smoked paprika
½ tbsp ground coriander
3 tbsp olive oil

FOR THE YOGURT & TAHINI WHIP (OPTIONAL – SERVES 2):

6 tbsp plain coconut yogurt
juice and zest of 2 lemons (buy
    organic and unwaxed if you
    can)
2 tbsp runny tahini
2 tbsp extra virgin olive oil
2 tbsp maple syrup

Preheat the oven to 200°C/180°C fan/gas 6.

Put the carrots, beetroots and celeriac on a large baking tray. Drizzle with olive oil, sprinkle with salt and pepper, and roast in the oven for 25–30 minutes, until the vegetables are tender but not mushy.

In the meantime, using a pestle and mortar or a spice grinder, bash the fennel and cumin seeds. Put them into a large bowl and add the walnuts, pecans, oats, pumpkin seeds, sesame seeds, smoked paprika, ground coriander and a pinch each of salt and pepper. Mix everything together, then pour over the olive oil and mix again.

Remove the baking tray from the oven and spread the crumble on top of the vegetables. Put the tray back into the oven for a final 10–12 minutes, until the crumble is golden brown.

If you want to make the whip, simply whisk all the ingredients together in a bowl until smooth and silky.

Serve the crumble as it is, or with the yogurt and tahini whip.

Summer Baked Beans

This recipe always brings back nostalgic memories of my Italian summers. Like many Italian recipes, this dish is wonderfully simple and built on exceptionally flavourful seasonal products. The cannellini beans have a delicate flavour, with an aromatic hint of sun-drenched oregano and thyme. White beans might not immediately strike you as a beauty food, but they are actually high in polyphenol antioxidants, which combat oxidative stress in your body and slow down ageing. They are also rich in protein, fibre, folate and zinc, that wonderful beauty mineral which helps to keep breakouts at bay.

For an easy dinner I often have this dish on its own with a drizzle of extra virgin olive oil and a slice of crunchy bread, but it's also great alongside my Red Pesto Traybake Veg Salad (page 181) or my Broccoli & Quinoa Tabbouleh (page 243).

SERVES 4 AS A SIDE

250g dried cannellini beans or
   500g cooked cannellini beans
1 white onion, finely chopped
2 red peppers, deseeded and cut
   into small pieces
200g cherry tomatoes, cut in half
2 garlic cloves, finely chopped
1 red chilli, finely sliced
a few sprigs of fresh oregano
a few sprigs of fresh thyme
1 tsp smoked paprika
3 tbsp extra virgin olive oil + extra
   to serve
1 tbsp tamari sauce
2 tbsp tomato purée
salt and pepper, to taste

If you are cooking your cannellini beans from dry, soak them in plenty of cold water for 8–12 hours. Drain, rinse, then put them into a large pot and cover them with water. Cook on a medium heat for 45–55 minutes, until soft but still holding their shape. To save time you can also cook them in a pressure cooker for 20–25 minutes.

Preheat the oven to 200°C/180°C fan/gas 6.

Once the beans are cooked, drain them and put them on a large baking tray with the chopped onion, peppers, tomatoes, garlic, chilli, oregano and thyme. Sprinkle with the smoked paprika, olive oil, tamari sauce and a generous pinch each of salt and pepper.

In a small bowl dilute the tomato purée with 100ml of water. Pour the tomato water on top of the beans and gently mix everything together. Cover the tray with kitchen foil and bake in the oven for 50 minutes. Remove the foil and bake uncovered for the final 15 minutes, until your beans are slightly crispy on top. Serve with a drizzle of extra virgin olive oil.

TIP
If you are short of time you can use tinned beans, but the texture might be a bit softer.

Super Green Dip

This is the perfect dip to up your plant-based protein and your greens at the same time. It's really vibrant, and extra creamy thanks to the buttery macadamia nuts. Peas, edamame and broad beans are all crammed with antioxidants, which help to protect your skin against free-radical damage for a dewy complexion. They are also all very high in fibre, which will keep you feeling fuller for longer and will contribute to regular bowel movement and detoxification. I often use this as a spread in sandwiches, or I add a dollop to a bowl of quinoa, roasted sweet potatoes and veggies, for a quick dinner.

MAKES 1 LARGE BOWL

100g frozen peas
100g frozen edamame beans
100g frozen broad beans
20g macadamia nuts or cashews
a small handful of fresh mint
    (about 5g)
a small handful of fresh coriander
    (about 5g)
3 tbsp extra virgin olive oil
2 tbsp lemon juice
1 garlic clove, crushed
salt and pepper, to taste

Put the frozen peas, edamame and broad beans into a large pan. Cover with boiling water and cook on a medium heat for 5 minutes until soft, then drain well and rinse them under cold water to stop the cooking process.

Put the peas, edamame and beans into a food processor, together with the macadamia nuts, mint, coriander, extra virgin olive oil, lemon juice, garlic and a pinch each of salt and pepper. Blitz until you have a fairly creamy purée. If you would like your dip a bit more runny, add a couple of tablespoons of cold water and pulse again. Taste and adjust the seasoning.

Store any leftovers in an airtight container in the fridge for 2–3 days.

Broccoli & Quinoa Tabbouleh

I know the idea of eating raw broccoli doesn't sound hugely appealing, but trust me – in this tabbouleh-style salad it really works. In fact, you won't believe how tasty it can actually be! The key is to make sure the broccoli florets are chopped to a super-fine consistency, so I would definitely recommend using a food processor for best results. The natural bitterness of the broccoli is beautifully balanced by the fruity flavour of the pomegranate, the fresh zing of the herbs and the rich nuttiness of the almonds and pumpkin seeds. This salad is not only packed with cart-loads of flavour but it is also a powerhouse of antioxidants, minerals, vitamins and healthy fats, which will feed and nourish your skin with every bite. I like to have it alongside some grilled tofu or tempeh, but thanks to the quinoa, it is also really filling on its own.

SERVES 4 AS A SIDE

70g quinoa
1 head of broccoli, florets only
40g pumpkin seeds
40g almonds, roughly chopped
1 medium carrot, peeled, chopped
   into thin matchsticks, then cut
   into small pieces
½ a red onion, finely chopped
seeds of ½ a large pomegranate
a small bunch of fresh parsley
   (about 30g), chopped
a small bunch of fresh coriander
   (about 30g), chopped

FOR THE DRESSING:
80ml extra virgin olive oil
juice of 1 lemon
1 tsp Dijon mustard
1 tsp maple syrup
salt and pepper, to taste

Cook the quinoa according to the packet instructions. In the meantime, make the dressing. Simply put all the ingredients into a bowl and mix well.

Put the broccoli florets into a food processor and pulse for few seconds until they have the consistency of rice. Set aside.

Put the pumpkin seeds and chopped almonds into a dry pan and toast them on a medium heat for around 5 minutes, until fragrant.

Using a fork, fluff up the cooked quinoa and put it into a large bowl together with the broccoli 'rice', carrot, red onion, pomegranate seeds, chopped herbs and the toasted nuts and seeds. Pour the dressing on top and mix well before serving.

TIP
This is the kind of salad that stores well in the fridge for a couple of days, so if you have any leftovers pop them into an airtight container for a fast lunch the next day.

Roasted Cauliflower & Butter Bean Dip

This is a superb way to use cauliflower – it's so incredibly creamy thanks to the mix of tahini and butter beans, while the roasted shallots and spices gives it real depth of flavour. It's also a fantastic fuss-free recipe for sneaking extra cruciferous veggies into your diet. When cut or cooked, cauliflower, like broccoli and Brussels sprouts, produces a phytochemical known as indole-3-carbinol that supports healthy liver function, which is important for hormonal balance, meaning fewer breakouts! I enjoy this as part of a quick lunch with some toasted bread, slices of tomato and a little handful of rocket.

MAKES 1 LARGE BOWL

300g cauliflower, cut into florets
2 shallots, peeled and cut in half
a drizzle of olive oil, for roasting
½ tsp ground cumin
½ tsp ground coriander
1 x 400g tin of butter beans,
    drained and rinsed
2 tbsp runny tahini
2 tbsp lemon juice
2 tbsp extra virgin olive oil
salt and pepper, to taste

Preheat the oven to 200°C/180°C fan/gas 6.

Put the cauliflower and shallots on a large baking tray, drizzle with the olive oil and sprinkle over the cumin and coriander. Season with salt and pepper and toss everything together. Roast in the oven for 25 minutes, until the cauliflower is soft and slightly charred around the edges. Remove from the oven and let it cool down for 5 minutes.

Put the roasted cauliflower and shallots into a food processor with the drained butter beans, tahini, lemon juice and extra virgin olive oil. Pulse for few seconds until everything is well incorporated. Scrape down the sides, add 2 or 3 tablespoons of cold water, then blitz again until smooth and creamy. Taste and adjust the seasoning.

Store any leftovers in an airtight container in the fridge for 2–3 days.

Kale Pesto Dip

This recipe combines two of my favourite things: pesto and a creamy dip. It's fresh and tangy, with a radiant richness from the pine nuts. I have added some kale for a dose of skin-boosting vitamins A, E and C, as well as extra fibre and antioxidants. It's an unbeatable dip to add to virtually anything. It works really well with mixed roasted vegetables, or as a side in a big salad spread, and is brilliant as a dip with drinks before dinner when I have friends around.

MAKES 1 BOWL

25g pine nuts
20g kale, stems removed, leaves
    roughly chopped
20g fresh basil
1 x 400g tin of butter beans,
    drained and rinsed
1 garlic clove
2 tbsp lemon juice
2 tbsp nutritional yeast
2 tbsp extra virgin olive oil
salt and pepper, to taste

Put the pine nuts into a dry pan and toast them on a medium heat for 5 minutes, until fragrant. Remove from the heat and set to one side.

Put the kale and basil into a large heatproof bowl and cover them with boiling water. Blanch them for 30–50 seconds, then fish them out of the water and transfer them to a bowl filled with ice cubes and cold water. Once they have cooled down, squeeze out all the water and put them into a food processor, together with most of the toasted pine nuts and all the other ingredients. Blitz until everything is well combined. While the food processor is running, add 3 tablespoons of cold water and keep blitzing until you have a creamy and smooth consistency.

Taste and adjust the seasoning. Serve topped with the remaining toasted pine nuts.

Store any leftovers in an airtight container in the fridge for 2–3 days.

Beetroot Dip with Smoky Almond Crunch

I must admit that one of the main reasons I make this dip very frequently is because it's just so pretty. That vibrant pink colour will brighten up any table, making the perfect dip for sharing platters and gatherings. Beetroots are absolutely loaded with antioxidants and vitamin C, which are both crucial for boosting collagen production and defending our skin against premature ageing.

The smoky and salty almonds balance perfectly the subtle sweetness of the beets and they also provide a hefty dose of healthy fats and UV-rays-protecting vitamin E. They also elevate this dip to something extraordinary, so please don't skip them!

MAKES 1 BOWL

1 medium beetroot, trimmed,
    peeled and cut into quarters
a drizzle of olive oil, for roasting
1 x 400g tin of cannellini beans,
    drained and rinsed
1 tbsp runny tahini
2 tbsp extra virgin olive oil
juice of ½ a lemon
1 garlic clove, finely chopped
salt and pepper, to taste

FOR THE ALMOND CRUNCH:

40g almonds, halved
½ tbsp olive oil
½ tbsp tamari sauce
1 tsp maple syrup
1 tsp smoked paprika

Preheat the oven to 160°C/140°C fan/gas 3 and line a baking tray with parchment paper.

Put the beetroot quarters on an unlined baking tray. Drizzle with olive oil, sprinkle with a pinch of salt, and roast in the oven for 30 minutes, until the beetroot is soft when pierced with a fork.

Spread the almonds on the lined baking tray and roast in the oven alongside the beetroot for 8–10 minutes. Remove from the oven, leaving the paper on the tray, and put the almonds into a frying pan on a medium heat together with all the other almond crunch ingredients. Mix everything together so the almonds get evenly coated, then cook them for 5 minutes, until all the liquid has evaporated and the almonds are sticky and glossy. Transfer back to the parchment paper and leave to cool.

Put the cooked beetroot into a food processor with the cannellini beans, tahini, 2 tablespoons of extra virgin olive oil, the lemon juice, garlic and a generous pinch each of salt and pepper, and blitz until smooth and creamy. While the food processor is running, add 1 tablespoon of cold water through the feeding tube for an extra silky consistency. Taste and adjust for seasoning.

Serve the beetroot dip with the smoky almonds on top. Store any leftovers in an airtight container in the fridge for 2–3 days.

Zesty Broad Bean Salad

This is my favourite salad to make when spring arrives. It's a splendid dish to celebrate the warmer days, as it's zesty and refreshing – perfect as a side dish or filling enough as a main. Broad beans or fava beans are one of those totally underrated legumes which actually packs a substantial nutritional punch. They are rich in plant protein and other important nutrients, including thiamin, vitamins K and B6, copper, selenium, zinc, potassium and magnesium, all incredible for boosting skin health and promoting shiny hair and strong nails.

To make the most of this wonderful legume I would recommend removing the outer skin, which is often quite bitter and stringy while the bean inside is deliciously sweet and buttery. This is the kind of salad that keeps well, making it the perfect lunchbox addition.

SERVES 4 AS A SIDE

90g quinoa
500g frozen/fresh broad beans, podded
20g pumpkin seeds
20g sunflower seeds
1 large tomato, seeds removed and finely diced
2 spring onions, finely chopped
20g fresh mint leaves, finely chopped
20g fresh dill, finely chopped

FOR THE DRESSING:

4 tbsp extra virgin olive oil
1 garlic clove, crushed
1 tsp Dijon mustard
juice and zest of 1 lemon (buy organic and unwaxed if you can)
1 tsp maple syrup
salt and pepper, to taste

Cook the quinoa according to the packet instructions. Once cooked, fluff it up with a fork and leave it to one side.

Put the broad beans into a large pan and cover with plenty of boiling water. Cook on a medium heat for 5–8 minutes, until the beans are soft. In the meantime, put the pumpkin seeds and sunflower seeds into a dry frying pan and toast them on a medium heat for about 5 minutes, until the pumpkin seeds start to pop.

Drain the broad beans and rinse them under cold water to stop the cooking process. Peel off the skins and put them into a large bowl with the cooked quinoa, diced tomatoes, spring onions, mint and dill. Mix everything together.

To make the dressing, put the oil, garlic, mustard, lemon juice and zest, maple syrup and a generous pinch each of salt and pepper into a bowl and whisk together. Pour the dressing over the salad and serve with the toasted seeds sprinkled on top.

The salad will keep well in the fridge for up to 2–3 days.

Pepper & Sun-dried Tomato Dip

Sun-dried tomatoes are one of those ingredients that instantly inject so much life into any recipe – even just a few of them can really make all the difference. I love their rich flavour alongside the natural sweetness of the roasted pepper, cannellini beans and cashews, creating a creamy and hearty dip. Peppers are famously abundant in collagen-boosting vitamin C, but they are also a great source of B vitamins, for healthy hair, and anti-ageing beta-carotene, for firm, elastic skin. I love a big spoonful of this with a bowl of roasted veggies and brown rice, or serving it with crunchy crudités and my Rosemary & Fennel Buckwheat Crackers (page 219).

MAKES 1 BOWL

1 red pepper
1 garlic clove, skin on
olive oil, for drizzling
60g raw cashews
1 x 400g tin of cannellini beans,
    drained and rinsed
4 sun-dried tomatoes
2 tbsp lemon juice
1 tsp white miso paste
½ tsp smoked paprika
1 tbsp extra virgin olive oil
salt and pepper, to taste

Preheat the oven to 200°C/180°C fan/gas 6.

Put the whole pepper and garlic clove on a baking tray, drizzle with olive oil and sprinkle with a pinch of salt. Roast in the oven for 30 minutes, until the pepper is really soft and squishy.

In the meantime, put the cashews into a large heatproof bowl and cover with plenty of boiling water. Leave them to soak for 30 minutes.

Remove the pepper from the oven and allow it to cool down. Once it has cooled enough to handle, remove the stalk, skin and seeds (they should all come off really easily). Squeeze out the garlic flesh from the skin.

Put the roasted pepper and garlic flesh into a food processor together with the drained cashews, beans, sun-dried tomatoes, lemon juice, miso paste, smoked paprika and extra virgin olive oil. Blitz until smooth and creamy. Taste and adjust the seasoning.

Store any leftovers in an airtight container in the fridge for 2–3 days.

Fermented Foods

My first introduction to fermented foods was when I was five, when my dad started experimenting with making his own sauerkraut. I still remember the piercing smell (to put it kindly) when he used to open his jars of fermented cabbage at the dinner table. My brother and I would make all kinds of disgusting faces and noises and he would just laugh, saying: 'I know I am on to something, one day you will buy these in all the trendy shops.' Well, as with many other things, my dad was right. Fermented foods have seen a huge increase in popularity in recent years and it's a trend I can firmly stand behind. Despite its new-found fashionable status, fermentation certainly isn't novel. It has been around for thousands of years, used as a way of preserving food. Almost all traditional cultures have a history of fermentation. From kimchi in Korea and natto in Japan to sauerkraut in Europe, fermented foods have been a food staple way before you saw them on the shelves of your local health food shop.

Fermentation is a natural process through which microorganisms like yeast and bacteria convert carbs – such as starch and sugar – into alcohol or acids. The alcohol or acids act as a natural preservative and give fermented foods a distinctive funk and tartness. Fermentation also promotes the growth of beneficial bacteria, known as probiotics.

While you can take probiotic supplements, I personally find fermented foods a cheaper and more effective way of looking after your gut, as you can also get a good dose of prebiotics at the same time. Prebiotics (not to be confused with probiotics) are non-digestible plant fibre and are resistant to digestion in the stomach and intestines, but are metabolized by the bacteria in the colon. They help promote the growth and activity of beneficial bacteria and encourage a decline in pathogenic bacteria. Fermented foods can therefore be a naturally rich source of prebiotics and probiotics, which work together to support our health.

A number of health benefits are associated with fermentation. In fact, fermented foods are often more nutritious than their unfermented form.

Improve digestive health: The probiotics produced during fermentation can help restore the balance of friendly bacteria in your gut and may alleviate digestive problems.

Support your immune system: Due to their high probiotic content, fermented foods may support your immune system and reduce the risk of infections in those with healthy immune systems. Those with compromised immune systems are advised to avoid probiotics. Many fermented foods are also rich in vitamin C, iron and zinc – all of which contribute to a stronger immune system.

Make food easier to digest: Fermentation helps break down nutrients in food, making them easier to digest. They may also improve bowel function and promote regularity, improving our detoxification capacity.

I know from personal experience that fermenting your own foods can feel really alien, but trust me when I say it's incredibly easy and so much more affordable than buying them from the store. The first time I had a go at making my own kraut I gave my dad a call to ask for his recipes. He talked me through the process and one hour later I had two jars of kraut happily fermenting away. The recipes in this chapter are ones which my dad and I have mastered over several years of attempting to ferment pretty much anything! I love to add a forkful to my Happy Skin bowls, to salads or just on top of a regular avocado toast. The serving suggestions are endless.

Before you get started, here are some of my top tips to make the process easier and foolproof:

- You can use any jars that you have in your cupboards – just make sure the lids close properly and are not rusty. Sterilize jars and lids in boiling water to make sure no bacteria will interfere with the fermentation process.

- If for any reason your kraut doesn't produce enough liquid (purple cabbage, for example, is really sturdy and tends to produce less), you can add some salted water to make sure the vegetables are still submerged in the brine. Simply bring 200ml of water to the boil, add 1 teaspoon of sea salt and whisk until it is dissolved. Let the water cool down completely, then pour enough over the kraut to submerge it, and close the lid.

- Leave your kraut to ferment in a cool, dark place for 2 to 4 weeks to let the fermentation process do its magic. I usually love the flavour after 2 weeks, but I would encourage you to taste the fermented vegetables as you go along. The longer you let the kraut ferment, the stronger and sourer the flavour will be. After 2 weeks, taste the kraut and if you are happy with the flavour, place it in the fridge. Once the jars are in the fridge the kraut will keep for up to 4 months.

- If any white mould appears during the fermentation process you can just scrape it off. The pieces underneath will still be safe to eat. In the unlikely case that your sauerkraut grows green mould, the whole batch should be thrown away.

These recipes are designed to help you create probiotic- and nutrient-rich foods in the comfort of your kitchen. I promise you, if you can stand a bit of a whiff, once you start fermenting you will never want to stop!

Apple, Fennel & Dill Kraut

This is the first kraut that I ever made and the one I keep going back to over and over again. I love the sweetness of the apple combined with the aniseed punch of the fennel and the bitterness of the cabbage – it just works. It's crunchy and tangy, the perfect addition to any salad.

MAKES A 1.5-LITRE JAR

1 large white cabbage, roughly 1.15kg, any outer leaves and core removed

1 large head of fennel, roughly 270g

1 apple, roughly 130g, core removed

30g sea salt

1½ tbsp caraway seeds

2 garlic cloves, crushed

5g fresh dill, roughly chopped

Wash the cabbage and fennel well, then slice them really finely. For ease and speed, I would recommend using a mandoline. Slice the apple into thin matchsticks.

Put the cabbage, fennel and apple into a large bowl and mix in the salt. Massage the salt vigorously into the cabbage for roughly 5 minutes.

Try to squeeze out as much liquid as possible from your veg. Make sure to keep the liquid, as that's going to be the brine in which the kraut will be submerged. If you are concerned about

your cabbage not releasing enough liquid, just keep massaging. This stage can usually take anything between 8 and 10 minutes. Cover the bowl with a tea towel and let it sit for 1 hour.

Add the caraway seeds, garlic and fresh dill to the bowl and massage everything for another 5 minutes. At this point the volume of the veg should have reduced dramatically and you should have a lot of liquid at the bottom of the bowl.

Transfer the kraut into the sterilized jar and pack it in very tightly, using your knuckles to push it down. Make sure you leave about 5cm of space at the top, then pour in the liquid from the bowl. Once the fruit and veg are fully submerged under the brine, close the lid of the jar and leave it to ferment in a cool, dark place for 14 days, then taste it and if you're happy with the flavour, transfer it to the fridge.

During the fermentation process some of the liquid might spill out, so I would recommend placing a bowl or a plate underneath the kraut jar. The kraut will keep in the fridge for up to 4 months.

Apple Kimchi

I have to admit it took me a while to get my taste buds accustomed to the fieriness of kimchi. Now I am obsessed with it, and I have it with pretty much anything! From a regular avocado toast, to leftover rice or even in soups (check out my Kimchi Noodle Soup on page 156), kimchi can really bring any dish to life, adding tons of flavour. If you are struggling to handle spicy foods, I would recommend halving the quantity of the gochugaru. You can really tweak it and cater it to your personal taste. Source gochugaru chilli powder and daikon (a white radish, also called mooli) at Asian supermarkets, or online.

MAKES A 2-LITRE JAR

1 head of garlic
15g fresh ginger, peeled and grated
40g gochugaru chilli powder
2 Chinese cabbages (about 2 medium), core removed
3 medium carrots, roughly 300g, trimmed
1 medium daikon radish, roughly 300g, trimmed
4 spring onions
1 apple, roughly 130g, core removed
35g salt

Put all the garlic cloves, ginger and chilli powder into a food processor and pulse for few seconds until you have a crumbly paste.

Wash the cabbages, carrots, daikon and spring onions well, then slice really finely. A mandoline for the cabbage and daikon and a julienne peeler for the carrots makes things simple. Slice the apple into thin matchsticks.

Put the cabbage, carrot, daikon, spring onion and apple into a large bowl and mix in the salt. Add the chilli paste and massage everything vigorously for roughly 5 minutes. Try to squeeze out as much water as possible from the veg. Make sure to keep the liquid, as that's going to be the brine in which the veg will be submerged. If you are concerned about your cabbage not releasing enough liquid, just keep massaging. This stage can take anything between 8 and 10 minutes. Cover the bowl with a tea towel and let it sit for 1 hour.

Massage everything for another 5 minutes. At this point the volume of the veg should have reduced dramatically and you should have quite a lot of liquid at the bottom of the bowl. Kimchi usually doesn't release quite as much water as other krauts, so don't worry if you don't have quite as much.

Transfer the kimchi into the sterilized jar and pack it in very tightly, using your knuckles to push it down. Make sure you leave about 5cm of space at the top, then pour in the liquid from the bowl.

Once all the veg are fully submerged under the brine, close the lid of the jar and leave it to ferment in a cool, dark place for 14 days, then taste it and if you're happy with the flavour, transfer it to the fridge.

During the fermentation process some of the liquid might spill out, so I would recommend placing a bowl or a plate underneath the jar. The kimchi will keep in the fridge for up to 4 months.

Golden Turmeric & Carrot Kraut

This kraut is sensational on a bleak winter day. It is a ray of sunshine in a jar. I adore the combination of carrots and cabbage with the wonderfully warm flavour of the turmeric, ginger and caraway seeds. The turmeric gives the kraut a gorgeous bright yellow colour, not to mention a little nutrition boost.

MAKES A 1.5-LITRE JAR

1 large white cabbage, roughly 1.15kg, any outer leaves and core removed
3 large carrots, roughly 350g, trimmed
10g fresh ginger, peeled and grated
5g fresh turmeric, peeled and grated
30g sea salt
1 tbsp caraway seeds
1 tbsp fennel seeds
2 garlic cloves, crushed

Wash the cabbage and carrots well, then slice them finely. A mandoline for the cabbage and a julienne peeler for the carrots can make it quick and easy, but watch your fingers.

Put the cabbage, carrots, ginger and turmeric into a large bowl and mix in the salt. Massage the salt vigorously into the cabbage for roughly 5 minutes. Try to squeeze out as much liquid as possible from your veg. Make sure to keep the liquid, as that's going to be the brine in which the kraut will be submerged. If you are concerned about your cabbage not releasing enough liquid, just keep massaging. This stage usually can take anything between 8 and 10 minutes. Cover the bowl with a tea towel and let it sit for 1 hour.

Add the caraway seeds, fennel seeds and garlic to the bowl and massage everything for another 5 minutes. At this point the volume of the veg should have reduced dramatically and you should have a lot of liquid at the bottom of the bowl.

Transfer the kraut into the sterilized jar and pack it in very tightly, using your knuckles to push it down. Make sure you leave about 5cm of space at the top, then pour in the liquid from the bowl.

Once all the veg are fully submerged under the brine, close the lid of the jar and leave it to ferment in a cool, dark place for 14 days, then taste it and if you're happy with the flavour, transfer it to the fridge.

During the fermentation process, some of the liquid might spill out, so I would recommend placing a bowl or a plate underneath the kraut jar. The kraut will keep in the fridge for up to 4 months.

Purple Beet Kraut

You just can't beat the vivid purple colour of this kraut. Just by looking at it, you know it is jam-packed with skin-glowing antioxidants. I absolutely adore the earthy taste profile of the beets with the slightly resinous and peppery flavour of the juniper berries. Because of its gorgeous pink colour, this is the perfect addition to make any bowl look instantly prettier (and tastier!).

MAKES A 1.5-LITRE JAR

1 large purple cabbage, roughly 1.15kg, outer leaves and core removed
350g beetroots (about 2 medium), trimmed
10g fresh ginger, peeled and grated
30g sea salt
1½ tbsp juniper berries
2 garlic cloves, crushed

Wash the cabbage and beetroots well, then slice them really finely. I would recommend using a mandoline for the cabbage and a julienne peeler for the beetroots.

Put the cabbage, beetroots and ginger into a large bowl and mix in the salt. Massage the salt vigorously into the cabbage for roughly 5 minutes. Try to squeeze out as much water as possible from it. Make sure to keep the liquid, as that's going to be the brine in which the kraut will be submerged. If you are concerned about your cabbage not releasing enough liquid, just keep massaging. This stage usually takes anything between 8 and 10 minutes. Cover the bowl with a tea towel and let it sit for 1 hour.

Add the juniper berries and garlic to the bowl and massage everything for another 5 minutes. At this point the volume of the veg should have reduced dramatically and you should have a lot of liquid at the bottom of the bowl.

Transfer the kraut into the sterilized jar and pack it in very tightly, using your knuckles to push it down. Make sure you leave about 5cm of space at the top, then pour in the liquid from the bowl.

Once all the veg are fully submerged under the brine, close the lid of the jar and leave it to ferment in a cool, dark place for 14 days, then taste it and if you're happy with the flavour, transfer it to the fridge.

During the fermentation process some of the liquid might spill out, so I would recommend placing a bowl or a plate underneath the kraut jar. The kraut will keep in the fridge for up to 4 months.

Sweets

I have always had the biggest sweet tooth. I am
the girl who would always pick a dessert over
a starter any time of the day. However, when I
embarked on my mission to clear my skin, I had
to sit down with my sweet tooth and have an
honest chat. I knew refined sugar had to go; no
more pastries for breakfast, no more half packets
of caramel digestive biscuits for dessert; and it had
to be goodbye to the two teaspoons of sugar in
my coffee as well. Saying that it took me a while
to adjust to this new, refined sugar-free lifestyle
is an understatement, but I am happy to say that
over time my palate has definitely changed and
I no longer get excited about sugar-laden treats.
However, I firmly believe in balance and in finding
a way of eating that supports your beauty and
health but is also enjoyable and fun.

"All these treats taste perfectly decadent and rich but are all made with wholegrain or nut-based flours and natural sweeteners."

The Happy Skin Kitchen philosophy is about skincare from inside, using nutrient-dense food to feed and nourish your skin with every morsel, but it is also about the pleasure of eating, so I absolutely do not deprive myself of desserts, cakes or sweets. The idea of life without a slice of cake or a cookie seems terribly gloomy and definitely not sustainable. That's why I started making my own better-for-your-skin treats and sweets. I still want something sweet and indulgent, which will satisfy my sweet tooth, but I now focus on nutritionally dense ingredients that will also feed my skin with minerals, antioxidants and vitamins. All these treats taste perfectly decadent and rich but are all made with wholegrain or nut-based flours and natural sweeteners. Unlike chemical sweeteners, glucose syrup and refined sugar, these sweet ingredients are less processed and closer to their wholefood state. This ensures they are mineral-rich and give you the maximum nutrients per mouthful. I balance these sweeteners with fats and proteins like coconut oil, nuts and seeds, nut butters and legumes. This not only adds nutrition but slows down the absorption of sugars, helping to reduce sugar spikes and energy dips.

MY FAVOURITE BAKING STAPLES

Sweeteners: My favourites are dates, maple syrup and coconut sugar, which have beauty benefits and a lower glycemic index than refined sugar. Maple syrup contains trace minerals such as zinc, iron and manganese. Coconut sugar is minimally processed and contains B vitamins and potassium. Dates, apart from having that decadent caramel flavour, are packed with fibre and are rich in protective antioxidants.

Wholegrain flours: Buckwheat and oat are my go-to flours, both naturally gluten-free and full of fibre, minerals and vitamins.

Chickpeas and chickpea water: I know you might not expect to find legumes in the sweets chapter, but chickpeas are super-versatile and are a wonderful staple to make anything fudgier, such as my Chocolate Cookie Dough Bars. Chickpea water (also called aquafaba) is almost like a magic ingredient, working as a natural egg replacer to make bakes fluffier and lighter.

Other dry goods: Nuts and seeds, nut butters, dark chocolate and raw cacao powder. Raw cacao powder is one of my favourite storecupboard ingredients and I use it in an array of recipes, from breakfasts and snacks to drinks and desserts. It's the unprocessed version of cocoa, so it's richer in antioxidants and minerals. Nuts and nut butters are a wonderful way to add skin-hydrating fats and also bring a delicious buttery flavour to the sweet party. For dark chocolate, I would encourage you to invest in the best quality you can afford, with a high percentage of cocoa (anything between 70 and 90 per cent) for a richer flavour and more goodness.

Caramel & Chocolate Ganache Pots

I know the idea of making caramel with chickpea water sounds incredibly odd, but trust me – aquafaba (chickpea water) is a magical ingredient. I love using aquafaba in baking as a binding agent instead of eggs, but it also works wonders if you are trying to make a plant-based version of a traditional meringue. In this recipe it creates an unbelievably fluffy and moussy consistency, and I promise you won't taste the chickpeas. These caramel and chocolate pots are spectacularly decadent and yet are made with minimal ingredients and no refined sugar! To create that indulgent caramel flavour, I have used Medjool dates, which are a wonderful source of magnesium, potassium and antioxidants such as flavonoids, carotenoids and phenolic acid, all very helpful when it comes to protecting your skin from oxidative stress. For the chocolate ganache, I would recommend using the best quality dark chocolate you can find. Its bitterness will balance the sweetness of the caramel and you will boost your minerals and antioxidant intake.

MAKES 4 SMALL POTS

5 Medjool dates, pitted
120g smooth and runny almond
    butter
50g coconut cream (the thick top
    part of a tin of full-fat coconut
    milk)
120ml chickpea water, from a tin
    (aquafaba)

FOR THE CHOCOLATE GANACHE:

90g good quality dark chocolate
    (I love to use 70% cocoa),
    roughly chopped
100g coconut cream

TIP
You can either use
shop-bought coconut
cream or chill a tin of
full-fat coconut milk in the
fridge overnight. Just scoop
out the solid layer on top
and use the rest of the
liquid in smoothies or
curries.

Put the Medjool dates into a heatproof bowl and cover them with boiling water. Soak them for 5 minutes, then drain them and with your hands squeeze out the excess water. Put them into a blender (you can also use a hand blender for this) with the almond butter and coconut cream. Blend until you have a sticky paste. Try to blend as much as possible so you don't have big chunks of dates.

Put the chickpea water into a clean bowl. With an electric whisk set at the fastest speed, whisk for at least 5 minutes, until the aquafaba starts to thicken up and resemble a thick and fluffy meringue consistency.

Very gently, fold the meringue into the almond butter paste until the two are very well incorporated. Don't overmix, as you want to maintain a fluffy consistency. Pour the mixture into 4 small glasses or jars, and place in the fridge to set for at least 6 hours, or even better overnight.

To make the chocolate ganache, put the chocolate and coconut cream into a heatproof bowl over a pan of simmering water on a low heat. As the chocolate melts, mix everything together until the two are well combined and the ganache has a silky and smooth consistency.

Allow the chocolate ganache to cool slightly before dividing it between the 4 pots. Put back into the fridge to set for another 30 minutes before serving.

Lemon & Coconut Loaf

Coconut and lemon is probably one of my favourite flavour combinations. It has that nostalgic feel of long summer days, warm sunshine and dips in the sea. I love the sweet tropical notes of the coconut, which are perfectly balanced by the tangy and zesty flavour of the lemon. Coconuts are rich in copper and iron, which help form red blood cells, as well as in selenium, an important antioxidant that fights free radicals and helps protect your skin from oxidative stress. To make this loaf extra nutritious, I have added buckwheat and ground almonds, which are both high in protein, fibre, vital beauty minerals and healthy fats. This loaf is absolutely delicious as it is, but sometimes I serve it with a dollop of coconut yogurt and my Raspberry Chia Jam (page 66).

MAKES 1 LOAF

250g buckwheat flour
50g desiccated coconut
150g ground almonds
2 tsp baking powder
1 tsp bicarbonate of soda
200ml maple syrup
50ml chickpea water, from a
    tin (aquafaba)
150ml oat milk
juice and zest of 1 lemon
    (buy organic and unwaxed
    if you can)
1 tsp vanilla bean paste
2 tbsp melted coconut oil

TO DECORATE (OPTIONAL):
pared or peeled lemon zest
toasted flaked coconut

Preheat the oven to 200°C/180°C fan/gas 6, and line a 23 x 13cm loaf tin with baking paper.

In a large bowl, mix together the buckwheat flour, desiccated coconut, ground almonds, baking powder and bicarbonate of soda.

In a separate bowl, mix together the maple syrup, chickpea water, oat milk, lemon juice, lemon zest, vanilla bean paste and melted coconut oil. Pour the wet ingredients into the dry and gently mix everything together. Don't over-mix the batter. When you don't see any more dry flour, stop mixing.

Pour the mixture into the lined tin and bake in the oven for 45 minutes, until golden brown around the edges. Remove from the oven and let the loaf rest in the tin for 10 minutes before transferring it to a wire rack to cool down completely, ideally overnight or for at least 2–3 hours.

Decorate with shards of pared or peeled lemon zest and toasted flaked coconut, if you like.

You can keep the loaf in an airtight container for 2–3 days, or alternatively you can cut it into slices and store them in a sealable food bag in the freezer for 3 months.

Almond Butter Cups

These are by far my favourite treat. They are super-easy to make and they require no baking. I love the crumbly base, the creamy almond butter layer and the fudgy chocolate topping – they are just bliss in every bite. I must admit, I do get ridiculously excited when I create a treat that tastes so indulgent and decadent and yet is made only with wholesome ingredients. These cups are high in fibre, thanks to the oats, and they are brimming with healthy fats and vitamin E to help your skin stay hydrated and protected from UV rays. I give these as presents for friends and they always turn out to be the best edible gifts.

MAKES 10 CUPS

FOR THE BASE:

80g pitted Medjool dates
75g ground almonds
65g porridge oats

FOR THE MIDDLE LAYER:

150g smooth and runny almond
    butter

FOR THE TOPPING:

1 x 400g tin of full-fat coconut
    milk, chilled in the fridge
    overnight
70g good quality dark chocolate
    (I love to use 70% cocoa),
    broken into pieces
2 tbsp maple syrup
1 tsp vanilla bean paste

TO DECORATE:

a sprinkle of flaked almonds
    (optional)

TIP
The leftover coconut water is perfect for adding to smoothies and drinks. Try my On-the-go Raspberry & Mint Chia Fresca (page 198).

Line 10 holes of a 12-hole muffin tray with muffin cases.

Put the dates into a heatproof bowl and cover them with plenty of warm water. Leave them to soak for 15 minutes.

To make the base, put the ground almonds and oats into a food processor and blitz until you have a crumbly flour. Add the soaked and drained dates and blitz again until you have a sticky mixture when pressed between your fingers.

Place about 2 tablespoons of the base mix in each muffin case and press down to even out the layer, then place in the fridge.

While the base is chilling, open the chilled coconut milk tin and carefully scoop out the solid white coconut cream into a heatproof bowl, reserving the liquid for another time (see tip). Add the dark chocolate to the bowl and place on top of a pan of simmering water on a low heat.

As the chocolate and coconut cream melt gently, whisk everything together until smooth and silky. Add the maple syrup and vanilla and stir to combine, then remove from the heat and leave to one side.

You are now ready to assemble the almond butter cups. Remove the muffin tray from the fridge and place about a tablespoon of the almond butter in the middle of each base. Then pour over the chocolate topping so that each cup is completely covered. Sprinkle with flaked almonds (if using) and place in the fridge to set overnight, or in the freezer for 1–2 hours.

The almond butter cups will keep in an airtight container in the fridge for up to 6 days.

Granola Cookies

These cookies are the perfect thing to grab and go with some fruit if you're rushing out of the door in the morning. The seeds mean they are bursting with skin-loving minerals and omega-3, and they are guaranteed to keep you feeling full until lunchtime thanks to the slow energy-releasing oats. I like to make a big batch of them on a Sunday so I know I have some nourishing bites on hand during the week, no matter how busy my schedule is.

MAKES 12–14 COOKIES, DEPENDING ON THE SIZE

100g jumbo oats
50g ground almonds
35g pumpkin seeds
35g sunflower seeds
35g hemp seeds
1 tbsp chia seeds
60g raisins
1 tsp baking powder
1 tsp bicarbonate of soda
10g solid coconut oil
3 heaped tbsp nut butter of your choice (I have used almond)
100ml maple syrup
1 tsp vanilla bean paste

Preheat the oven to 200°C/180°C fan/gas 6 and line a baking tray with parchment paper.

In a large bowl, mix together the oats, ground almonds, pumpkin seeds, sunflower seeds, hemp seeds, chia seeds, raisins, baking powder and bicarbonate of soda. Melt the coconut oil – I usually just put it in a small bowl in the microwave for 30–40 seconds.

In a separate bowl whisk together the nut butter, maple syrup, vanilla bean paste and melted coconut oil. Pour the wet ingredients into the dry and combine well until you have a sticky mixture. Using an ice cream scoop or your hands (wet them slightly so the mixture won't stick to your fingers), shape the cookie dough into 12–14 balls and flatten them on the parchment paper. Bake in the oven for 12–14 minutes until golden brown around the edges.

Remove the cookies from the oven and let them cool down for 15–20 minutes before serving. Store in an airtight container for up to 5 days.

Muesli Muffins

These mightily moreish muffins make the ultimate afternoon snack or on-the-go breakfast. Because of the oats, ground almonds and seeds, they are very high in fibre, which feeds our gut microbiome and also keeps us feeling fuller for longer. The mix of seeds adds a delicious crunch, but has important beauty minerals too. Sunflower seeds are brimming with selenium, great for repairing damaged cells. It also contains a high percentage of vitamin E, which is vital in the production of collagen and elastin. Pumpkin seeds are abundant in zinc, which has a wide array of beauty benefits such as lowering inflammation, fighting the bacteria that can cause breakouts and protecting the skin against free radicals. I love these muffins with a spoonful of almond butter.

MAKES 10 MUFFINS

150g oat flour
50g jumbo oats
90g ground almonds
2 tsp baking powder
1 tsp bicarbonate of soda
30g pumpkin seeds
30g sunflower seeds
2 tsp ground cinnamon
50g solid coconut oil
1 very ripe banana (around 90g peeled weight)
100ml maple syrup
100ml almond milk
60g raisins

Preheat the oven to 200°C/180°C fan/gas 6, and line 10 holes of a 12-hole muffin tray with muffin cases.

In a large bowl, mix together the oat flour, jumbo oats, ground almonds, baking powder, bicarbonate of soda, pumpkin seeds, sunflower seeds and cinnamon.

Melt the coconut oil. I usually put it into a bowl in the microwave for 1 minute.

In a separate bowl, mash the banana. Add the melted coconut oil, maple syrup and almond milk and mix everything together. Pour the wet ingredients into the dry and stir to combine. Fold in the raisins. Divide the batter between the muffin cases, about 2 tablespoons for each case, leaving a little space at the top as they will rise during the baking process.

Bake in the oven for 20–22 minutes, until risen and the tops are slightly golden brown. Remove the muffins from the oven and leave them in the tray for 10 minutes, then transfer them to a rack to cool down completely. Store in an airtight container for 3–4 days.

Chocolate Cookie Dough Bars

These are my box-set TV treat when I need that sweet hit of happiness. Chickpeas are my store-cupboard wonder ingredient because they are so versatile and can be used in savoury and sweet recipes. When you blitz them with creamy cashew butter, maple syrup and vanilla, they create the perfect cookie dough-like consistency which is even more delicious when sandwiched between a nutty layer at the bottom and a silky chocolate ganache on top. These bars have been one of my absolute top treats when the sugar craving strikes. Rich in antioxidants from the cacao and crammed with healthy fats from the nuts, they are also high in fibre and protein to truly satiate and please.

MAKES 12 X 5CM BARS

FOR THE BASE:
140g Medjool dates, pitted
100g ground almonds
3 tbsp raw cacao powder
1 tbsp melted coconut oil

FOR THE COOKIE DOUGH LAYER:
1 x 400g tin of chickpeas, drained
  and rinsed
4 tbsp maple syrup
100g nut butter of your choice
  (I love cashew butter for this
  recipe)
1 tsp vanilla extract

FOR THE CHOCOLATE GANACHE:
100g good quality dark chocolate
  (I love to use 70–80% cocoa),
  broken into pieces
100ml full-fat coconut milk,
  from a tin

Line a 23 x 13cm loaf tin with baking paper. Put the dates into a heatproof bowl and cover them with plenty of warm water. Leave them to soak for 10 minutes, then drain.

Make the base. Put all the ingredients into a food processor and blitz until the mixture sticks together when you press it between your fingers. Transfer to the loaf tin and spread it across the tin using your hands. Place it in the fridge to set while you are making the rest.

Wipe clean the food processor and put in all the ingredients for the cookie dough layer. Blitz until you have a fairly smooth consistency. You might need to scrape down the sides of the food processor and blitz again. Remove the tin from the fridge, then, using a spatula, spread the cookie dough layer on top of the base. Place the tin back in the fridge while you are making the final layer.

To make the chocolate ganache, put the chocolate and coconut milk into a heatproof bowl on top of a pan of simmering water on a low heat. When the chocolate starts to melt, whisk everything together and keep whisking until you have a smooth and silky chocolate sauce.

Remove the tin from the fridge and pour over the chocolate ganache. Shake the tin around to make sure the chocolate is evenly distributed. Place the tin back in the fridge for 1 hour to set, then cut into 12 even squares. Store in the fridge for up to 5 days or in the freezer for 3 months.

Blueberry & Lemon Muffins

These muffins are the perfect example of something wholesome yet utterly delicious. They are fluffy, subtly sweet and they only require a few simple ingredients. Blueberries are especially rich in a powerful type of antioxidant called anthocyanins. In addition to giving them a deep blue pigment, anthocyanins inhibit the breakdown of collagen, the protein that keeps skin plump and elastic. They are also a great source of vitamin C, which is vital for collagen production. Thanks to the oat flour and ground almonds, these muffins are also high in fibre and protein. Oats are also rich in B vitamins, which provide a host of benefits to the skin, not least in helping to combat skin diseases such as rosacea, acne and eczema. They're also a wonderful skin moisturizer. Vitamin B3 has been shown to improve the epidermis (outermost layer of the skin) in retaining moisture. These muffins are also an excellent breakfast-on-the-go for busy days or for when you need extra motivation to get up in the morning.

MAKES 12 MUFFINS

240g oat flour
100g ground almonds
100g coconut sugar
2 tsp baking powder
1 tsp bicarbonate of soda
a pinch of sea salt
120g jarred apple purée
juice and zest of 1 lemon (buy organic and unwaxed if you can)
100ml oat milk
2 tbsp melted coconut oil
1 tsp vanilla bean paste
150g fresh blueberries

Preheat the oven to 200°C/180°C fan/gas 6, and line a 12-hole muffin tray with muffin cases.

In a large bowl, mix together the oat flour, ground almonds, coconut sugar, baking powder, bicarbonate of soda and salt.

In a separate bowl, whisk together the apple purée, lemon juice, lemon zest, oat milk, melted coconut oil and vanilla bean paste. Pour the wet ingredients into the dry and gently mix until a thick batter forms. Stir in the fresh blueberries.

Divide the mixture equally between the 12 muffin cases, about 2 tablespoons to each case. Bake in the oven for 22–25 minutes, until golden on top and around the edges.

Remove from the oven, leave the muffins in the tin for 10 minutes to firm up, then transfer them to a rack to cool down completely.

The muffins will keep in an airtight container at room temperature for up to 3 days.

Hazelnut & Chocolate No-bake Tart

This tart is pure indulgence. It's rich, sumptuous and super chocolatey with a lovely nutty flavour, perfect for long dinners with friends. I absolutely adore the taste of the toasted hazelnuts with the sweetness of the coconut and the richness of the chocolate. It's pure heaven on a plate! Often chocolate is pictured as the ultimate unhealthy food, but did you know that cacao has more antioxidants than any other food? Yes, blueberries included! Chocolate with a big cacao percentage (look for at least 70 per cent) can help to boost skin hydration and reduce skin redness by increasing nutrients and blood supply to the skin. This tart is also ridiculously easy to make, and because no baking is required you can make it in advance and store it in the fridge for 2–3 days.

MAKES 1 X 23CM TART

FOR THE BASE:

150g pitted Medjool dates
120g hazelnuts + extra for
    decoration (optional)
70g porridge oats
2 tbsp raw cacao powder

FOR THE FILLING:

2 x 400ml tins of full-fat coconut
    milk, chilled in the fridge
    overnight
150g good quality dark chocolate
    (I love to use 70% cocoa),
    broken into pieces
3 tbsp maple syrup
1 tsp vanilla bean paste

Preheat the oven to 170°C/150°C fan/gas 3. Put the dates into a bowl and soak them in cold water for 20 minutes. Drain.

Put the hazelnuts on a baking tray and toast in the oven for 10 minutes. Remove from the oven and put into a food processor with the oats and cacao powder. Blitz for few seconds, until you have a crumbly flour. Add the soaked, drained dates and blitz again until the mixture sticks together when you press it between your fingers.

With your fingers, crumble the dough evenly over the base of a 23cm shallow non-stick loose-bottomed cake tin. Starting from the middle, press the mixture firmly and evenly into the tin, moving outwards and upwards along the sides of the tin. The harder you press the dough into the tin, the more likely it will hold together.

Place the tart in the fridge to set while you are making the filling.

Open the chilled coconut milk tins and carefully scoop out the solid white coconut cream into a heatproof bowl, reserving the liquid for use another time (see tip page 270). Add the dark chocolate to the bowl and place on top of a pan of simmering water on a low heat. When the chocolate starts melting, using a whisk to mix everything together, and keep whisking until you have a silky and smooth texture. Add the maple syrup and vanilla and stir to combine.

Remove from the heat and pour over the chilled tart base. Gently shake the cake tin around so the filling gets evenly distributed. Place the tart back in the fridge overnight to set, or in the freezer for 1–2 hours. When you are ready to serve, remove the tart from the tin. Place on a serving plate and sprinkle with the chopped hazelnuts (if using), then cut into even slices. Store in the fridge for 2–3 days.

Apple & Raisin Loaf

This is one of my go-to sweet loaves that I make on repeat because it is just so easy and versatile. Sometimes I have a slice (or two!) for breakfast, or sometimes I pop a slice in the toaster then load it with a dollop of almond butter for a sweet afternoon pick-me-up. I love using ground almonds in baking – it's such a nutrient-dense flour that's rich in fibre and protein. Almonds are rich in antioxidant vitamin E, which helps protect cells from oxidative stress caused by pollution, UV rays and other external factors. For example, one serving of 23 almonds provides 60 per cent of your daily recommended vitamin E needs. Almonds are also a solid source of copper, which helps maintain skin and hair pigmentation. I have used apple purée as a binding agent instead of eggs, but apples are also a great source of vitamin C and antioxidants. They contain pectin, which not only fills you up but is also a prebiotic which can help to feed the good bacteria in your gut. The addition of chickpea water might sound a bit off, but it's only there to make the loaf light and fluffy. I promise you won't taste it at all!

MAKES 1 LOAF

140g ground almonds
130g buckwheat flour
1 tsp baking powder
1 tsp bicarbonate of soda
1 tbsp ground cinnamon
a pinch of sea salt
320g jarred apple purée
50ml chickpea water, from a tin
    (aquafaba)
180ml maple syrup
2 tbsp melted coconut oil
2 tsp apple cider vinegar
2 tbsp plant milk of your choice
    (I have used oat)
50g raisins or sultanas

Preheat the oven to 200°C/180°C fan/gas 6 and line a 23 x 13cm loaf tin with baking paper.

In a large bowl, mix together the ground almonds, buckwheat flour, baking powder, bicarbonate of soda, cinnamon and salt.

In a separate bowl, mix together the apple purée, chickpea water, maple syrup, coconut oil, apple cider vinegar and plant milk. Pour the wet ingredients into the dry and gently mix everything together. Don't over-mix the batter, stop when you don't see any more dry flour. Fold in the raisins.

Pour the mixture into the loaf tin and bake in the oven for 45 minutes.

Remove from the oven and let the loaf rest in the tin for 10 minutes, then transfer it to a wire rack to cool down completely, ideally overnight or for at least 2–3 hours.

TIP
This loaf is suitable for freezing. Just cut it into slices and store in a sealable food bag for 2–3 months. You just need to toast it for few minutes.

Happy Skin Rituals & Beauty Practices

At the core of the Happy Skin Kitchen philosophy is a belief that food is a more powerful beauty tool than any skincare product or treatment. The nutrients in food are the building blocks on which your body relies to continually rebuild and repair. The quality of the foods you eat directly influences how well your body is able to support and maintain your skin. I believe we are what we eat. For me, the most profound and most impactful beauty practices will always be about spending time in the kitchen, creating meals with ingredients that support me in looking and feeling my best.

"The most wonderful aspect of these practices is the connection you cultivate with yourself."

Beauty will always start in the kitchen, but it is also about self-love and instilling rituals with a mind-body approach. It's about how I feel, as well as how I look. So, over the past few years I have also mastered making rituals and homemade beauty products which I'm confident have the power to give my skin that little extra care and attention that it sometimes needs. There are many magical ingredients in nature that have been proven to do wonders for our skin, hair and body, and I am passionate about discovering them and experimenting with them to create my own potions and lotions. I am not saying that these should replace your existing skincare routine – I still use various brands for my skin, body and hair care that I have researched from an ingredient and animal welfare point of view (I love REN for skincare and Faith In Nature for body and haircare). I simply regard these DIY beauty recipes as rituals of self-care and self-love. I find the process of making and using them very calming and grounding.

These Happy Skin rituals aren't just about physically looking your best – the most wonderful aspect of these practices is the connection you cultivate with yourself. I hope you can use them as tools for being more present and to take some time to show your skin and your mind some adoration and care. The almost meditative nature of these self-care practices is a gift that really keeps on giving. Whenever I feel stressed out, I always reach for my Lavender & Chamomile Sleep-aid Bath Salts, which have the power to leave me with a feeling of inner harmony and relaxation. And if I am feeling tired after a long day at work I always grab my Almond & Neroli Nourishing Body Oil, which feels so luxurious and leaves my skin soft and hydrated, while comforting my soul at the same time. The recipes you find in this chapter call for only a few ingredients and are easy to make, so you don't have to employ too much effort. Some of the recipes can also be tailored to your personal preference. For example, would you prefer my Coffee & Orange Energizing Body Scrub to be a bit more oily? Go for it! The ingredients are simple enough that you can tinker around and play with what suits you and your skin best.

It's worth noting that most recipes made with natural ingredients will keep for up to 3 days, excluding the body scrub and the oils, which will keep for up to 3 months. Always store your potions in an airtight container or jar for maximum freshness.

Oat & Yogurt Gentle Face Scrub

This scrub is super-gentle, hence it is suitable for all skin types. I know a lot of physical scrubs can feel very harsh for the delicate skin on your face – however, this scrub exfoliates dead cells without irritating the skin, all the while helping it to retain moisture. Oatmeal contains saponins, which act as a cleansing agent without stripping your skin and leaving it feeling tight. Almonds contain a good amount of vitamin E, which is not only an antioxidant but helps to prevent cell damage. I love using this scrub once a week to buff away dry, dead cells and leave my skin feeling soft, smooth and glowing.

MAKES 1 FACE SCRUB

½ tbsp ground almonds
½ tbsp oat flour
1 tbsp coconut yogurt

In a small bowl mix everything together until you have a paste. Rub gently onto clean skin. Wash it off and follow with your regular moisturizer or few drops of my Frankincense & Rosehip Anti-ageing Face Oil (page 290).

Frankincense & Rosehip Anti-ageing Face Oil

I have been experimenting with face oil blends for years, and this pairing is my firm favourite. Rosehip oil intensely nourishes the skin, improving the appearance of firmness and elasticity while promoting a more even tone. It also helps remedy dryness, blemishes, dull skin, fine lines and scarring. Frankincense, on the other hand, is wonderful for irritated or damaged skin. It restores the epidermis, calms the complexion and it also has powerful anti-ageing properties. I have added jojoba and vitamin E for extra hydration, and antioxidants for a luminous glow. You can use this oil morning and night as part of your skincare routine. I always take it with me when I travel, as it's sublime for keeping my skin moisturized during a long flight. It's also a treat to indulge in a prolonged face massage at night-time. It's an incredible soothing ritual that helps me wind down and prepare for a restful sleep.

MAKES A 30ML BOTTLE

½ rosehip oil
½ jojoba oil
6 drops of frankincense
    essential oil
4 drops of vitamin E oil

Fill up the bottle with half rosehip and half jojoba oil. Add the frankincense and the vitamin E oil drops, then seal the bottle and shake well.

To apply, pour 4 or 5 drops of the oil into the palm of your hand and massage onto clean and slightly damp skin. Rub gently on to your neck as well, until the oil is fully absorbed.

Turmeric Brightening Face Mask

Turmeric has a long list of skin benefits. It has great anti-inflammatory properties and is jam-packed with antioxidants, making it a wonderful skin ingredient to include in your diet and in your beauty routine. This mask can be used to help treat blemishes, pigmentation, and rough, dry skin. The turmeric and lemon have incredible brightening properties and the coconut yogurt is extremely nourishing and soothing. I use it once a week, usually at the weekend when I have some extra time to pamper my skin. By the way, your skin won't be left bright yellow by the turmeric! Just make sure you wash your face thoroughly afterwards.

MAKES 1 MASK

1 tbsp oat flour
2 tsp ground turmeric
2 tsp plain coconut yogurt
1 tsp grated lemon zest (buy organic
   and unwaxed if you can)

Put all the ingredients into a bowl and mix to make a paste. Make sure your hair is away from your face and avoid wearing any clothes that you love, because turmeric can stain fabrics really easily. Apply the mask to your face, using either your fingers or a clean makeup brush. Leave the mask on for 20 minutes, then wash it off. After drying your skin (I would use an old towel, as once again turmeric can stain anything), use your favourite cleanser to remove any extra turmeric left on the face. Follow with your regular moisturizer or a few drops of my Frankincense & Rosehip Anti-ageing Face Oil (page 290).

Clay & Tea Tree Purifying Face Mask

This detoxifying mask is great for fighting blackheads, minimizing pores and helping prevent breakouts. Bentonite clay gently draws dirt and impurities from the skin, leaving it feeling cleansed and refreshed. When it comes to fighting blemishes, tea tree oil is a powerful natural ingredient, as it absorbs excess sebum without over-drying. I always reach for it when my skin starts to look a bit congested. It has the power to leave me with dreamy-looking skin that feels deeply cleansed and balanced.

MAKES 1 MASK

1 tbsp bentonite clay (I usually buy it online)
1 tbsp oat flour
5–6 drops of tea tree essential oil

Put the clay powder and oat flour into a bowl and mix together. Add the tea tree essential oil and 2 or 3 tablespoons of water. Mix everything together until you have a paste.

Before you apply the mask, I would recommend washing your face using your favourite cleanser. Once your skin is nice and clean, apply the mask using either your fingers or a clean makeup brush. Leave it on for 10–15 minutes, then gently wash it off. Afterwards apply your regular moisturizer or a few drops of my Frankincense & Rosehip Anti-ageing Face Oil (page 290).

Almond & Neroli Nourishing Body Oil

This was one of the first DIY beauty products I ever made. Homemade body oils are very simple to make, and you can customize them with whatever scent you like. I absolutely adore neroli oil for its multitude of beauty benefits. It helps with scarring, stretch marks and dry skin, and it has a wonderful soothing scent. The almond, jojoba and vitamin E make this oil a luxurious and deeply hydrating body treatment to intensively nourish and replenish your skin, plus help calm your mind. I use this daily after my shower. For best results, I would recommend applying it to damp skin to lock in more moisture.

MAKES A 100ML AMBER GLASS BOTTLE

almond oil
jojoba oil
10 drops of neroli essential oil
10 drops of vitamin E oil

Pour almond oil into your bottle to come halfway up. Add the same amount of jojoba oil, until the bottle is almost full. Add the drops of neroli and vitamin E oil. Close the bottle and shake well.

To apply, pour a generous amount of the oil into the palm of your hand and massage onto damp skin.

Coffee & Orange Energizing Body Scrub

You can't beat a good body scrub for removing dead skin cells and giving you instantly softer skin. Making your own DIY body scrub is super-easy, cheap and – if you are a coffee drinker – is a great way to upcycle coffee grounds that otherwise would go to waste. The level of antioxidants in coffee increases as it's brewed, so repurposed coffee is even better for your skin. Coconut oil is mixed with the coffee to provide lots of moisture to your skin as you scrub, so you will be left smooth, soft and glowing. I love adding orange essential oil for its energizing scent, but you can use any essential oil of your choice.

MAKES ENOUGH FOR 1 FULL BODY SCRUB

100g solid coconut oil
100g ground coffee
10 drops of orange essential oil

Melt the coconut oil. I usually place it in the microwave for 1 minute, or melt it in a small pan on a low heat for 2–3 minutes. Put all the ingredients into a bowl and mix everything together. Apply the coffee body scrub in the shower, on wet skin. Scrubbing should be done in a circular motion, with attention given to dry rough areas. Rinse with warm water and pat dry with a towel after use.

Store any leftover scrub in a sealed jar for up to 2 months.

Lavender & Chamomile Sleep-aid Bath Salts

Having a hectic work schedule, fitting in exercise, cooking and finding time to do the things you enjoy, all amounts to a busy and sometimes stressful life. It can be difficult to wind down at the end of the day, which means many of us go to bed with a frenetic mind, and our sleep is disrupted. A night of quality sleep is worth a hundred eye creams. During sleep, your skin's blood flow increases, and the organ rebuilds its collagen and repairs damage from UV exposure, reducing wrinkles and age spots. Enriched with chamomile and lavender, these Sleep-aid Bath Salts are ideal for relaxing the body and mind and for soothing aches and tired muscles. Frankincense, peppermint and lavender help to encourage deep, restorative sleep.

**MAKES AROUND A
1-LITRE JAR**

500g Epsom salts
15 drops of frankincense
    essential oil
10 drops of peppermint
    essential oil
50g dried lavender flowers
50g dried chamomile flowers
250g Himalayan salt

Fill the jar halfway full of Epsom salts. Next, add the frankincense and peppermint oil. Put the lid on and shake well to combine. Remove the lid and add the dried lavender and chamomile flowers. Put the lid back on and shake again. Fill up the rest of the jar with the Himalayan salt. Give it a final vigorous shake and it's ready to be used next time you want to have a relaxing bath.

Index

Acknowledgements

First and foremost, I would like to say thank you to my incredibly supportive online community. To all of you who made my recipes, watched my videos, left comments, emailed me or sent me a DM of love and encouragement when I needed it the most; I wouldn't have my dream job and this book if it wasn't for your continuous support. I poured my heart and soul into this book and I genuinely hope it will have a positive impact.

To my mum and dad for being the best parents I could have ever wished for. Dad, you taught me to love and respect the natural world, you instilled in me a passion for eating in a way that nourishes our body and respects the planet, too. Mum, for making me the strong and resilient woman I am today. Grazie mille.

To my life-long friends Carlos, Roel and Karin for always being there for me. I will always be so grateful for your love, laughter and silliness, which has always made me smile even during the most stressful times (and there have been plenty!).

To my friend Rebecca for helping me bring to life some of the recipes with the most vibrant photography. Thank you for always telling me 'you got this' when I really felt I was losing my sanity testing a recipe for the millionth time.

My wonderful editor Katya for believing in this book from the get-go, for all your enthusiasm and for making it all possible. Thank you also to Georgina, James, Sim and the rest of the HarperCollins team for all the work you put into this book to make it look absolutely stunning and better than I could have ever imagined.

And last but in no way least, thank you to Sam, my partner in crime and the love of my life. For proofreading this book about 100 times, your sound advice and putting up with me during the whole process. I know I have been a real nightmare at times but I wouldn't have been able to do it without your support and endless cups of tea. You are always pushing me to be the best version of myself and give me the confidence to chase all my dreams. Thank you.

About the Author

Born and raised in rural Bologna, Elisa moved to London in 2008 to follow her dream of working in fashion, gaining roles at Harrods and Aquascutum. During this period of her life, she began to suffer from hormonal acne.

No lotion, cream, pill or treatment seemed to cure her issues, so Elisa set about on a life-changing mission to change her skin from the inside out. Thus began a plant-based journey of discovery, which saw Elisa create a whole new diet for herself packed with foods to help repair, regenerate and replenish her skin, and sharing her recipes, successes and struggles online.

Elisa now works full-time on Happy Skin Kitchen and provides daily recipes and inspiration to over 300,000 followers across her growing Instagram, YouTube and TikTok channels. She lives in South London with her fiancé and their four cats.